BIOG ? ...
CW01642803

STRENGTH THROUGH ADVERSITY

A story of overcoming a life-changing injury and triumphing over adversity

DARREN EDWARDS

Copyright © 2023 by Darren Edwards

All rights reserved.

No part of this publication may be reproduced, distributed, or transmitted in any form or by any means, including photocopying, recording, or other electronic or mechanical methods, without the prior written permission of the publisher, except in the case of brief quotations embodied in critical reviews and certain other noncommercial uses permitted by copyright law.

ISBN Ebook: 978-1-7392830-0-1
ISBN Paperback: 978-1-7392830-1-8

Dedicated to the memory of
Raymond Edwards (1956 – 2021).

Loving father to me and my sister Eve Edwards,
and husband to Julie Edwards.

We miss you.

CONTENTS

PREFACE

This was it. The moment that my life would end. As I tumbled uncontrollably down the exposed rockface, I came to the heart-breaking realisation that there was nothing I could do to change the course of events already in motion. The base of the towering cliff was more than 120ft below me and closing fast. Even if I survived a fall of this magnitude, I would land on the jagged rock fragments of a steep scree slope. I believed that all hope was lost. It's a scary thought knowing that your last desperate shouts for help may ultimately be in vain. Only fate would decide when my story came to an end.

My longstanding thirst for adventure had led me to this life-altering moment. As a boy, I discovered a copy of *Touching the Void* in my school library and became captivated by tales of daring, sacrifice, and the life-or-death pursuits that defined so many pioneers of high-altitude mountaineering. I soon became inspired by the wild, rugged mountains of North Wales and spent every waking moment exploring them alongside my best friends. I'd never fooled myself that there wasn't an element of calculated risk as I pushed my limits, rockface by rockface, mountain by mountain. But it was an addictive, exhilarating pursuit of self-discovery.

Hurtling down the sheer cliff of World's End toward my climbing partner below, seconds seemed to last an eternity. Life wasn't flashing before my eyes, but it was suddenly put into sharp perspective for the first time. God, I'd never see Ellie again, my loving family, the friends I'd forged unbreakable bonds with. The promise of life would be left unfulfilled. So many dreams would now not come to pass – climbing Mount Everest, serving as part of the Special Forces Reserve, travelling the world.

Three words clung desperately to the frayed edges of my consciousness as I came close to blacking out: "Please don't die."

Life hung in the balance…

1

THE PROVING GROUNDS

I stood shoulder to shoulder with the remaining recruits. There were just 19 of us now, a tiny fraction of the 150 who had started, whittled down by the sheer magnitude and severity of the task we sought to achieve. Selection for the Special Forces Reserve is a war of attrition with both the mind and body – a price that not all were willing, or able, to pay. Only once we had proved ourselves determined enough, fit enough, and resilient enough over the windswept mountains of the Brecon Beacons mountain range in Wales (known affectionately as the "hills" phase by recruits), would we begin to learn the skills and tactics necessary to be part of the SAS(R). For the last six months, I had spent most weekends battling against the clock, and invariably against the elements, to prove that I had what it took to be part of this illustrious regiment. There was now one final punishing test ahead of us – the infamous "Endurance March".

We stood in the pitch black of a moonless January night. The freezing, driving sleet pounded against our bodies as we stood motionless, waiting to set off into the mountains above. The only reprieve from the engulfing darkness came from the dim headtorch of the Chief Instructor standing in front of us. "You know what tonight is," he said calmly to the group.

"This is the start of the longest day of your lives. If you want it bad enough, you'll find a way to keep going until the end." It was 23:00. We would have 22 hours to navigate 64 kilometres over the highest peaks of the Brecon Beacons carrying 75lb in our bergen (the weight of a seven-year-old child). Endurance came at the end of two continuous weeks of punishment we had known as "Loadstone" and then "Test Week". I waited to set off into the void of darkness in front of me, the weight of my bergen already cutting painfully into the top of my bruised shoulders. I'd made it this far. I sure as hell wasn't going to quit now.

"Edwards!" barked the Chief Instructor. I shuffled forward. "Off you go. Good luck," he said, noting the time of my departure on his clipboard.

I crossed the rutted track and plunged into the night. The six-figure grid reference I'd been given for my first checkpoint was over two thousand feet above. If I was to successfully make it to each checkpoint, I'd need to ensure that my night-time navigation skills were flawless. With my bearing set to the first trig point on the summit ridge above, I began to ascend the steep ridgeline to Twyn-Du. In the distance, I could see the faint outline of the recruit ahead of me. "Stay on him," came my self-directed rallying call. The temperature had continued to plummet overnight, and as I began to ascend the steep ridgeline, the driving sleet turned to a biting snow blizzard. Hypothermia would be the ever-present enemy – just waiting for us to make a simple error in our navigation or a lapse of judgement.

It took me an hour to reach the first of Endurance's summits, Craig y Fan. The horizontal blizzard had reduced visibility to no more than a few feet. With no visual cues to reaffirm my heading, I had to trust the bearing on my compass and my interpretation of the contoured landscape on my map. Winter selection is undoubtedly considered the toughest course, not only because of the adverse mountain conditions but also because of the short daylight hours. I caught up with the recruit ahead of me, who had become disoriented in the whiteout. He was about to head north towards a section of cliffs. Calling out through the wind, I got his attention and motioned in the direction of west. It was Clint, one of the closest friends I'd made on the course, who was also from the same unit as me. Recruits weren't meant to move together in pairs or small groups, but we took our chances together as we cautiously moved westward, avoiding a drop of eight hundred feet just to our right.

We followed the top of the mountain plateau for the next four kilometres. Heavy snow continued to fall, disguising icy pools of water dotted around us. On several occasions, my feet plunged unexpectedly into bitingly cold, knee-deep puddles. I was conscious that we needed to make up time now there was relatively flat ground ahead of us. "Let's get a bit of a shifty on?" I shouted through the driving wind to Clint. I quickened my stride, and we broke into a slow jog over the icy ground. The wind was horrendous as we doggedly approached the summit of Fan y Big. We were over halfway to the first checkpoint at the summit of the iconic Pen y Fan but first there was a precarious 650-foot descent to navigate through soft snow. There wasn't time to be overcautious, so I started my descent in earnest, leaning backwards and using my rifle as a crutch on the slope above me. With the very next step, I lost my footing and began to slide down the hill at a gathering pace. I turned onto my stomach and used my rifle as a makeshift ice axe to bring myself to a stop. Clint plodded down towards me, a smirk on his face as he joked, "Calm down mate, it's not

Mount Everest!"

Reduced to a slow plod, my legs straining under the weight of my bergen, I ascended the iconic east ridge of Pen y Fan. We'd spent countless hours being beasted up and over its steep face for the last six months, and I found strength knowing that this would be one final, symbolic ascent. The checkpoint was a small, green tent located ten or so metres from the summit cairn. Approaching alone, I took a knee outside the tent, its zip firmly closed in the beating wind. I called out my identification details to the Directing Staff inside, "Edwards, 42, Blue." In return, I was given a new six-figure grid reference, before setting back off into the darkness in search of the next RV point. It was freezing cold in the middle of that January night. I was alone once more, jogging down the mountain track as I headed for the valley floor. I'd stashed a Snickers bar in the front of my jacket pocket to help keep my energy levels up, but as I slung my rifle under my arm to undo the wrapper, it quickly became apparent that the bar was frozen solid. The SAS were looking for soldiers who could think on their feet and be adaptable, so I took the bold decision to put the frozen block down my compression shorts to defrost – which came as an abrupt shock to my genitals!

The dim, yellow headlights of the army trucks glistened in the falling snow as I made my way down to the roadside checkpoint. Approaching from the rear of the vehicles, I could see two recruits sitting, demoralised, in the back of the cabin, their bergens on the floor, and wearing a fresh pair of dry kit not covered by a sheet of ice. A small part of me envied them. But they were a harsh reminder that if it wasn't the for brutal attrition of fighting to survive in these conditions, the demons inside my head would be my undoing, as they had been for these recruits. I knew that I was roughly a quarter of the way through, about 16 kilometres in, and I'd averaged just under four kilometres an hour – my target for the last two weeks, and better than perhaps expected in these conditions. It was 03:30. The sun wouldn't begin to rise for at least another four hours.

I was now entering prime real estate for rolling an ankle as I slogged through terrain besieged with cut tree trunks and "moon grass" – melon-sized lumps of grass despised by recruits. I'd decided to contour south around the summit of the next mountain I would need to climb, Fan Fawr, located 1,000 feet above. I'd hoped to save time by avoiding the steeper option of summiting to the north, but I already knew that I'd made a mistake. I floundered through endless boggy, peaty terrain. My knees began to feel the strain as I frequently lost balance, the weight of the heavily laden bergen pulling me towards the ground. I could see the faint silhouette of a recruit on the ridgeline above me. Frustrated, I doubled my efforts to make up for my lapse in judgement and to hunt down the recruit in front of me. Finally, I reached the long, gradual spur that would lead me to the summit of Fan Fawr. The wind was horrendous, even down at the foot of the mountain. But, at that moment, the Chief Instructor's words drove me forward: "If you want it bad enough, you'll find a way to keep going until the end."

The slow incline to the summit of Fan Fawr strained my already tight calves and with every step the weight of my bergen seemed to increase. Approaching the summit plateau, I had a decision to make. My next checkpoint was just four kilometres away, south of the mountain to my west, Fan Llia. But if I headed straight for it, I'd have to descend the steep, western slope of Fan Fawr before making another leg-burning climb up the eastern face of Fan Llia. Alternatively, I could stick to high ground and avoid dropping down into the valley.

It would be more than double the distance, but if I could force myself to run, I'd ultimately save time (and energy). The lack of ambient light, coupled with the stinging sleet, made navigation more challenging. But, if I kept the low ground to my left, I knew I was headed in the right direction.

Two hours passed by in something of a laboured monotony as I forced myself to keep running across the snow-covered landscape. My mind was focussed on the goal ahead, on how good it would feel to complete the final victory kilometre to the waiting trucks. I couldn't live in the moment, apart from keeping on top of my navigation, due to the extreme cold and fatigue. Finally, I descended to the checkpoint, located five metres into a small woodblock. Once more, I crouched next to the tent and gave my details to the waiting DS, before heading in the direction of the halfway turnaround checkpoint.

The slow, spectacular winter sunrise came as a welcome relief from the hours spent navigating in the darkness. In the distance ahead, I could see a recruit struggling to walk, stumbling with every other step. I quickened my pace and soon caught up to him. It was Seth, one of the guys I'd formed a close friendship with and with whom I'd trained outside of selection. "Mate, what the hell happened?" I asked as I saw the expression of anguish and pain on his face.

"I rolled my bloody ankle on a hidden tree stump as I left the last checkpoint. I don't think I can keep going, mate," he responded. "I've got no chance of making it to the end at this pace," he said, and I could hear the defeat in his voice.

I couldn't see him fail; we'd come through far too much together and I cared as much about his success as I did my own. "Come on Seth, let's do this together. You can't give up now." I stayed by his side until we made it to the halfway RV. The other recruits I could see were all eating frantically, getting the calories their bodies desperately needed before shuffling back onto the trail. Seth urged me to start the final 32 kilometres without him. "Just don't quit," were my last words as I headed off into the wilderness once more. I doubted that he would make it any further. It had taken 10 hours to reach the halfway point.

Under different circumstances, I could have been forgiven for marvelling at the raw beauty of the landscape I was moving across: imposing peaks, deep ravines, and a patchwork quilt of flowing streams. But I was headed toward a part of the mountain range that had claimed the souls of countless recruits before me. Known as "VW (Voluntary Withdrawal) Valley", it was steep, difficult underfoot, and 48 kilometres into Endurance. Facing the prospect of yet another leg-burning climb, it is the point where many recruits are broken by exhaustion and the demons in their heads. I chucked a handful of Haribo into my mouth and begrudgingly began to tackle the ascent. My whole body was feeling the cumulative strain of two weeks of relentless punishment. As I finally cleared the summit, I paused for a moment in front of a rocky mural of Edward Maher, one of three recruits who lost their lives in the blistering heat of the summer selection course six months earlier. It was a stark reminder of the lurking, ever-present risks of exhaustion, hyperthermia and hypothermia.

The clock ticked on. I'd been on the go for more than 14 hours by the time I reached the boggy plateau above VW Valley and darkness had begun to fall once more. I'd only seen two recruits in the past three or four hours, otherwise I'd felt very alone. At the next RV, I gave my details and got my next grid reference, but as I went to leave the DS called me back, "Edwards, before you go," came the call from within his tent, and as I turned, he passed a chocolate biscuit through the tent's entrance. "Keep it up, you're near the front of the pack." A little taken aback by an unfamiliar warmth from one of the DS, I took the biscuit gratefully before heading off into the mist. There were still two checkpoints to go, 15 kilometres more before I could rest. I was cold and dehydrated, quite literally running on empty.

My pace began to falter. No longer was I able to run along the flatter sections of the terrain. I'd been reduced to a slow plod, my head bowed, just trying to keep one foot moving in front of the other. A handful of recruits passed me in the darkness, each time slamming a dent into my morale. Clint caught up with me; the last time we'd seen each other was on the summit of Pen y Fan 10 hours earlier. We headed to the penultimate checkpoint together before he surged ahead. I felt like the walking dead. Suddenly, I heard a whispered shout of "Daz!" from behind. I turned to see Seth striding towards me, very much still alive despite his ankle. I couldn't believe it. Before I could even ask how on earth he was still managing to keep going, he answered my question. "Mate, Tramadol is a beautiful drug!" Together, we headed for the final RV point.

Talybont Reservoir marked the end of Endurance. Our final kilometres were spent descending through thick pine forest, the dark expanse of water shimmering in the moonlight. I'd entered something of a delirious state, not sure how I was still managing to move forward. It was desire, grit, and stubborn determination alone that drove me on. Eventually, we made it across the reservoir. The headlights of the waiting trucks shimmered on the water. There were just 400 metres left, but with every two steps, I had to pause with my hands on my knees, totally drained. I stumbled across the line, 21 hours after setting off at 23:00 the previous night, to a simple but oh-so gratifying, "Good job Edwards," from the Chief Instructor.

It was over. I'd done it. A warm feeling of pride washed over me, and even better, I saw Seth stagger across the finish line as well. We had passed the mountain phase of SAS(R) selection.

2

LOST IN THE CLOUDS

Ever since picking up a copy of *Touching the Void* by Joe Simpson from the dusty confines of the sixth-form library, I became captivated by tales of daring, sacrifice and the life-or-death pursuits that defined so many pioneers of high-altitude mountaineering – the likes of George Mallory, Sir Edmund Hilary and Reinhold Messner. Their stories told of total belief in the ability to overcome seemingly insurmountable odds, unfathomable grit, determination and, ultimately in some cases, total sacrifice. As an unremarkable teen from Shropshire lacking in self-confidence and seeking a higher sense of purpose in life, it was these stories of intrepid expeditions and ground-breaking adventures that inspired me to be more.

New passions led, in turn, to new connections. I met a kindred spirit in Matt Luxton, a fellow student from my sixth-form college in Shrewsbury. Our friendship flourished in the mountains of North Wales as we tackled one wild, windswept peak after the next, battling against the elements and ourselves. We found a camaraderie in being roped together, working up a rock face or mountain, not as individuals but as a team. It was an unparalleled experience. The more time I spent surrounded by the eternal beauty of the mountains, the more I came to truly understand who I was as a person, and that I was capable of far more than the self-limiting beliefs I'd always harboured had led me to believe.

When asked, "Why do you climb?", George Mallory, the early pioneer of expeditions to Mount Everest, who died in 1924 on its North Face whilst trying to be the first to summit, simply responded, "Because it is there." For me, climbing captured the allure and mystery of life. Standing at the base of an imposing sun-baked cliff or the foot of a snow-covered gulley in the depths of winter, whether I succeeded or failed depended on my ability to remain mentally in control. To steal just a single moment at an elusive summit, having discovered the boundless nature of my own limits, was exactly why I climbed. There is also something special about friendships that are forged in the mountains, sometimes referred to as the "fellowship of the rope", whereby you implicitly and unquestionably entrust your life into another's hands.

It was this unrelenting pursuit to redefine my own limits that led me to the jaw-dropping, grandeur and beauty of the tallest mountain in Western Europe, Mont Blanc, in the summer of 2012. Alongside Matt, I overcame adverse weather conditions, spine-tingling rock falls through the Grand Couloir part way up the mountain, and the emotional burden of risking serious injury and death toward the summit ridgeline. The mountain had forced me to take a hard, honest look at myself. But I emerged with a renewed appreciation of how striving for a goal, and pushing beyond my current abilities, was the secret to my personal growth.

A couple of years had passed since Matt and I had climbed Mont Blanc together. When the opportunity arose to climb the second-tallest mountain in Western Europe, we jumped at the chance. Standing at 15,203ft, Monte Rosa sits on the Italy-Switzerland border and is a collection of ice-covered peaks soaring higher than 13,000ft. The sheer 8,000ft eastern wall of the mountain massif was almost Himalayan in size. From our base in the Italian village of Alagna Valsesia, we committed ourselves to the mountain, hoping for safe passage up its exposed slopes and glacier in pursuit of that fleeting moment when we could stand at the summit and gaze across the valleys below.

On the morning of our climb, a series of cable cars took us high into the mountains above Alagna Valsesia. To our north, the striking outline of the Monte Rosa massif dominated the skyline. We had good visibility of what would be our first target summit, Piramide Vincent at 13,800ft. The rising sun cast a beautiful, warm orange glow on its towering south face. Whilst the climbing season was beginning to open, there was still considerably more snow on the mountain than we had expected. Our moments of greatest vulnerability would be as we traversed the exposed knife-edge ridgeline between Piramide Vincent and the tallest summit, Dufourspitze, at 15,200ft. As we exited the top cable car station at Punta Indren, I strapped crampons to my mountaineering boots and unclipped one of the ice axes to hold in my right hand. Taking the first step on the slope ahead, I heard the familiar crunch of fresh snow beneath my feet. Exchanging a quick smile with Matt, I joked, “Race you to the top?”

The first section of our climb led us on a prolonged traverse to the Refuge Mantova, a mountain hut nearly 1,000ft above. We clipped gratefully onto a prepared line as we began to navigate an awkward section of mixed rock and snow. Above, I could see the silhouetted outline of two climbers moving across the ridgeline towards the refuge. The rising sun continued its gradual arc through the clear blue sky, glancing off the tips of jagged peaks as far as the eye could see. We moved lightly, undeterred by the weight of the packs, filled with all the necessary survival essentials we carried. After two hours of gradual climbing, we enjoyed a moment of rest and basked in the warm sun outside the Mantova refuge. Some 500ft above us was the precipitous Gnifetti Refuge, beyond which we intended to make camp for the night. The Gnifetti sat impossibly perched atop an exposed section of a ridgeline, its slender wooden structure hugging the rock tightly. We pushed forward, following a faint set of tracks in the snow, as we headed further up the mountain and to the far side of the refuge.

All too seldom in our modern lives do we stare in wonder at the natural beauty before us. Yet, as I summited the ridgeline on which the Gnifetti perched, I found myself speechless at the sight before me. The sprawling expanse of the mountain's glacier stretched in front of us as far as the eye could see, intricately scarred by deep ravines and crevasses. The sunlight overhead only seemed to emphasise the untold depths of these dark fissures. Fortunately, our line of ascent would take us away from the worst of it, but by no means entirely clear of danger. Clipping into the next fixed line, I abseiled a short distance to where we would set up our tent for the night, in the shadow of the refuge above. Gorging ourselves on a wheel of cheese from Alagna that night, we reflected on a successful day's work and bedded down as the temperature outside began to drop.

I slept restlessly. The temperature continued to plummet through the early hours of the morning to -25C. The constant shifting of the glacier emitted an unnerving cacophony of cracks and rumbles. And, as daylight began to break, I realised there was an unforeseen, potentially hazardous, complication… I couldn't see properly. I tried desperately to fully open my eyes but could only squint (at best). My face felt badly swollen and tender, as if I'd gone 12 rounds with a heavyweight boxer. "Matt, wake up!" I shouted in panic. "Mate, seriously, I think there's something really wrong with my face and eyes," I continued as I pulled at his sleeping bag. He turned over slowly to face me, and once his eyes had adjusted to the light, he just stared in shock for a few seconds before bursting out laughing.

"Mate," he exclaimed, "look at your face. You look like Kim Jong Un!" I reached clumsily for my phone and flicked the camera to selfie mode. I stared at the screen in utter disbelief, unable to comprehend that the image I was looking at was me. My cheeks and brow were badly swollen, so much so that I did look unnervingly like the North Korean dictator. I'd somehow had a freak reaction to the extreme cold overnight, and my face had swollen in quiet protest. Acknowledging that it wouldn't be safe to continue ascending in my current state, we retreated to the warmth of the Gnifetti refuge.

Fortunately for my pride, the refuge's only occupants were its French caretaker and a Nepalese cook. Even then, I couldn't avoid the inevitable, "What happened to your face?" in a thick French accent. From the relative warmth and comfort of the refuge, we watched as the weather outside deteriorated. Strong winds raced down from the summits above, colliding with the refuge and engulfing us in snow. Nicolas, the caretaker, offered us a bed for the night in the spacious refuge, which we accepted without hesitation. With zero phone signal or Wi-Fi, and with no other trappings of modern-day life, Matt and I settled down at the kitchen table for our first match of chess, followed by the only other game on the refuge's sparse games shelf – Yahtzee!

For the next two days, the mountainside was mercilessly ravaged by fierce winds and blizzard conditions. Any attempt to leave the refuge and ascend would be foolhardy – and we weren't yet prepared to give up on the summit. The intensity of the wind was like nothing I'd experienced before. That is the thing about mountains, they answer to no higher authority, they are impersonal and unforgiving. As the hours ticked by slowly and my ability to play chess refused to improve, our unplanned respite from climbing the mountain had allowed my face to return, almost, to its former size. Had it not been for the whiteout conditions, I could imagine the view from the Gnifetti of the glacier below and the summits above would have been truly spectacular.

I woke early on the fourth day to sunlight pouring into our cramped room through the horizontal window at the top of the cabin. I sprinted half-naked down the corridor to the emergency exit doorway, to be greeted by a clear blue sky and a mountainside positively sparkling in the sun's rays. After a thumbs up from Nicolas and a report of three positive weather forecasts, we geared up in the modestly sized boot room, bumped fists and headed for the summits high above.

It wasn't long before the reality of our situation dawned on us. The storm had dumped significant quantities of fresh, loose powder on the mountainside, effectively meaning that we would be climbing in risky winter conditions. Crevasses were increasingly likely to be covered in snow, making them harder to detect as we moved across the areas we'd identified as being dangerous. Once more, we roped together, trusting each other with our lives. We tied several overhand knots in the short line between us, which would help to act as an emergency break if one of us were to fall unexpectedly into a waiting crevasse. We were very much alone on the mountain as we began to ascend from the haven of the Gnifetti.

Now at the foot of the glacier, Matt took the first shift in front as we looked to cut horizontally across the steep slope.

My legs sank with each step to my knees; even as I tried to trace each of Matt's steps, it was a long, slow slog. Piramide Vincent loomed majestically above, its summit touched by the sun, a light wind blowing snow from its summit. I called ahead to Matt to let me take the next shift up front. Swapping over a few moments later, and as Matt caught his breath, he simply said, "Mate it's gopping." It was now my turn to be the human-powered snow plough. The gradient began to steepen as we reached the base of the imposing cliff that Piramide Vincent towered 2,000ft above. I began to carve a zigzag pattern up the slope, trying to expend less energy than tackling it head-on. Conditions underfoot started to deteriorate fast and despite my best efforts, our pace began to slow noticeably. My legs sank further and further into the fresh snow, and any semblance of rhythm had long since been lost. "It's like wading through treacle!" I shouted over my shoulder as I wiped the sweat from my brow and unzipped my jacket.

Three hours since we'd left the comfort of the Gnifetti, we were just 800ft below our first target summit, but we were entering the heart of crevasse territory. In every direction, I could see dark depressions in the snowline, the unknown depths of fissures in the glacier lurking beneath them. We probed our path forward, meandering carefully through the dangerous landscape. My heart was pounding, my mind thinking about nothing other than safely leading us through this minefield. Mercifully, after three hours, we finally began to crest the rocky summit ridgeline leading to Piramide Vincent. Gleefully approaching the summit, it was quickly apparent that the clear forecast we'd been given for today's weather had been a little optimistic. Before we had time to debate whether to push on or turn back, visibility began to drop, dramatically. At 13,800ft, and with a crevasse field to navigate between us and safety, we were engulfed at the beginning of a fresh snowstorm. Summiting was out of the question.

Despite my alarm, I was confident that we could navigate our way back to safety. The lack of visibility, coupled with freshly falling snow, made retracing our steps an increasingly futile mode of navigation – nothing looked familiar. A daunting, menacing atmosphere seemed to descend around us, weighing us down even further. Twenty minutes passed at an agonisingly slow speed. The loose tension on the rope reassured me that Matt was still with me but suddenly, a sharp and heavy pull on the rope pulled me backwards. "Brace! Brace! Brace!" came Matt's panicked shout behind me as a snow bridge over a crevasse collapsed beneath his weight. "Hold me there!" he called. I sank instinctively to my knees and buried my ice axe deep in the snow. I could hear his heavy breathing through the wind, coupled with the occasional curse, as he used his ice axe to extricate himself from the crevasse. Fortunately, one of the overhand knots we had tied in the rope had dug into the edge of the crevasse, stopping him from falling any further into the ice coffin.

Thick fog continued to plague our descent. I was now relying on a map and compass bearing to navigate our way back to the refuge. Thank God for the skills I'd picked up in Selection, I thought to myself midway through our descent. I began to open my stride up, convinced that we would soon be able to see the refuge through the improving visibility now that we were off the upper slopes. But the longer it took to materialise, the more doubt began to creep in. Had I taken a wrong bearing?

"There it is!" came the shout from Matt behind as he spotted the unmistakable outline of the wooden building upon its rocky throne, more majestic than ever before. A wave of relief washed over me, and with a new lease of life in our weary legs, we forged on until we had clambered back up to the wooden gangway of the Gnifetti. Turning to look at Matt for the first time since he'd emerged from the crevasse, we shared a collective sigh of relief as we puffed out our cheeks and embraced warmly. Collapsed side by side on a snowbank outside the refuge, we gazed back up the mountain and traced our steps until they became obscured by mist. Matt looked across to me and joked, "Well that was fun, fancy doing it again tomorrow?" We burst into uncontrolled, unadulterated laughter. Our friendship had certainly been forged in adversity and could always be trusted to lead us on an exhilarating, adrenaline-pumping escapade.

With snow continuing to fall, and a flight back to the UK in two days' time, there was only time to thank Nicolas for accommodating us before savouring one last look at the refuge and heading back down the mountain to Alagna Valsesia. George Mallory once famously quoted, "It is not the mountain we conquer, but ourselves." Although we had not summited the mountain on this occasion, I had indeed conquered any remaining lack of faith in who I was as a person and any lingering doubt as to how mentally strong and resilient I could be.

3

THE LAST PATROL

Only a handful of capable, determined and highly self-motivated soldiers remained at the end of the mountain phase of Selection to join the SAS Reserve. The regiment's selection process methodology was more than simply identifying the naturally fittest, strongest recruits. I'd already seen enough of these individuals give up and voluntarily withdraw in the mountains to know that physical fitness wasn't a critical success factor. Only once your body had been pushed to its physical limits, and when there was nothing left in the tank but determination, grit and pure desire, could the regiment begin to unearth the key quality they were looking for most – mindset.

At this stage we parted ways with the regular soldiers we'd shared the hills with for the last two weeks, as they would soon be headed off to Belize for the jungle phase of their selection process. Those attempting to join the SAS(R) had six months of weekends ahead of us to learn the specialist skills required, before an intensive two-week-long "Battle Camp" where our skills and character would be tested under exhausting, relentless pressure. Again, there was a mental component being tested, not just physical. Continuation training would prove to be a very different and much tougher beast altogether.

I stood to attention in the sparse drill hall of the main barracks. Emblazoned high on the wall above were the values that had forged the ethos and history of the SAS since its formation in the deserts of North Africa in 1941: humility, discipline, humour, a classless society and the unrelenting pursuit of excellence. It would be against these values, as well as the ability to learn quickly, to operate under pressurised conditions as a team and as an individual, and the ability to demonstrate controlled aggression, when needed, that we would either succeed or fail. In the mountains, we were trying to be "the grey man" and to slip through without drawing unwanted attention from the DS. Now, it was up to us to prove to them that they could soldier alongside you, trusting you implicitly to do the job at hand.

The pace of our continuation training weekends was fast and furious. We would need to master what the DS referred to as "green army" skills, such as section attacks, individual fire and movement and field craft – all at an accelerated rate before we could move on to learn the skills specific to our special forces unit. It would be on these specialist skills that most of our time would be spent. Contact drills, close target recces (CTRs), observation posts (OPs), snap ambushes, navigating through enemy territory – the pace was relentless and the learning curve steep. On top of becoming proficient in the various standard operating procedures (SOPs), we would also be expected to master a new weapon system each weekend and within 24 hours be expected to be able to operate, strip, reassemble, and pass a weapon-handling test. Only 11 recruits from 23SAS remained. Clint and Seth stood alongside me with those who remained.

My journey to Battle Camp didn't start as I'd intended. My lack of previous military experience quickly became apparent, particularly when compared to other recruits, such as Clint, who had already served in the regular army, parachute regiment, or with the marines. Physically, I was more than capable and robust enough to deal with the unrelenting pace and rigorous demands of what was being thrown at us, but I struggled to assimilate everything we were learning quickly enough to the elevated standard that was expected. Mid-way through our continuation training package, and with a couple of months yet to go until Battle Camp, four of the eleven remaining recruits were sent back and ordered to restart the process. I was one of the four, as was Seth.

Being cycled back to the beginning of the next course was a bitter pill to swallow and meant that I'd say goodbye to the lads I'd gone through hills with. Nevertheless, I was self-aware enough to acknowledge the fact I was behind the curve. Embracing this failure as an opportunity to learn and re-address my areas of weakness, I committed myself to bouncing back stronger. With the benefit of more experience and an additional Green Army training course under my belt, I returned both more confident and competent in my ability to pass the course. Six months later, as temperatures across the UK plummeted in January, I was in the back of our military transport headed to Battle Camp to prove that my place belonged with 23SAS.

The Warcop Training Area is a huge, undulating expanse in Cumbria within which the British Army conducts much of the training for its infantry units. It would be home for the first week of Battle Camp where our live fire manoeuvres as an individual, a four-man patrol, and an eight-person section, would be tested under the most strenuous circumstances. All assessments would be conducted using live ammunition, as we had grown accustomed to throughout our six months of training. Any slip-ups or mistakes had the potential to be deadly.

The pace of that week was relentless. Through freezing temperatures, and with snow steadily falling around us, we fought as an eight-person section up a steep incline, our legs burning as we aggressively closed on the "enemy" under the cover of suppressive fire from either Alpha or Bravo team. Or we crept through a narrow valley as a four-man patrol before encountering the enemy force, at which point we had to extricate ourselves from our vulnerable position. As soon as we had cleared the enemy position, or retreated to a safe distance, and as we paused to catch our breath with our hearts pumping furiously, we would just have time to refill the magazines for our C8 assault rifles and Light Machine Gun (LMG) before encountering a fresh scenario. Despite the gruelling pace on the ranges, from sunup to sundown, and with every step carefully watched by the lurking DS, I held my position, proudly going into our final assessment – patrol week.

We were now moved into our small four-man patrols and would be operating as an independent, self-contained unit for the coming operation. With my adrenaline surging, we sat in front of the Chief Instructor as he briefed us on the mission-specific details for the week ahead. The scenario for the exercise was simple: we would be inserted deep within enemy-held territory and would need to navigate our way to a target location, at which point we would build a covert observation post (OP), and conduct a close target recce (CTR), before regrouping with the other two patrols to form a joint assault plan. The Patrol Commander (PC) for our patrol was Kev, a hard-as-nails ex-Royal Marines Sniper who had transferred to the Army Reserve. I would be the patrol's Lead Scout, responsible for navigating our team to the target without detection and through deep forest. The pressure was well and truly on.

It was 01:00. The ground was thick with snow and the temperature had plummeted in the night to zero degrees. We travelled in the back of an unmarked truck under the cover of darkness to an intersection between two narrow roads, approximately 12 kilometres from our target. I made one final cursory check of my equipment: ammunition in my front pouches, waterproof map in my left thigh pocket, 140lb bergen behind me. The vehicle came to a stop and the driver banged on the metal partition behind him – time to go. We silently exited the back of the truck and took up an all-around defensive position as the vehicle left. Darkness enveloped us. Soon all was silent, save for the noise of the wind blowing through the trees. Signalling the patrol to follow me, we disappeared into the forest.

The terrain underfoot was difficult. As we moved slowly through the dense pine forest, exposed roots and tree stumps formed constant trip hazards. In the dim ambient light of the crescent moon, it was all but impossible to avoid the occasional stumble. The weight of my bergen cut sharply into my shoulders. Loaded with ammunition, claymores, rations, cold weather gear, as well as digging and construction materials for the patrol to build its OP, I was carrying almost double what I had carried on Endurance. Slowly, as the hours ticked by, my adrenaline began to wear off. Navigation was incredibly difficult. With no natural features and no meaningful natural light, I was reduced to working from compass bearings and distance to get us onto the target.

Static from the radio headset suddenly crackled quietly in my ear. "Daz, let's find somewhere we can make camp until first light," came Kev's voice. I led the patrol on a short loop so that we could set a snap ambush to make sure that our tracks weren't being followed. Once Kev and I had set up a claymore covering the entrance to our camp, we settled down for the next few hours as we rotated the role of "stag" through the patrol every 45 minutes. I didn't sleep. It was too cold, and I was too on-edge in anticipation of what was to come. Before I knew it, the winter sun had begun its low arc through the sky. It was time to move out and close distance to the target location nine kilometres away.

Time passed slowly, as did the kilometres. We only emerged momentarily from the depths of the forest so that I could take a knee, remove the map from my thigh pocket, and calculate our next bearing, before we plunged back into it again. We discovered enemy activity at the edge of the forest line, so we made sure to keep our distance as we moved forward, unseen. Although we kept our movement slow but constant, it was easy to become dehydrated. Occasionally, we would re-group in all-around defence so that the patrol could briefly eat and rehydrate. Snow continued to fall, settling in thick drifts on our bergens, and the temperature remained rooted to zero degrees. Before too long, the winter darkness began to descend once more. With light fading, we stopped short of the target to regroup, get our kit out and equipment sorted to build a covert sub-ground observation post from where we would watch the target location for the next three to four days.

"Let's prepare to move to our OP location," came the call from Kev, breaking the silence. Conversations had been kept to a minimum – only those that were mission critical. I headed out, with the rest of the patrol spaced evenly behind me. Our chosen route led us up a long, slow incline to the top of a treeline overlooking the target. Despite the weight on my back, my legs felt strong. I began to crest the top of the slope, flat ground ahead of me. I walked past a fallen pine tree, its roots exposed to the air when suddenly my left foot dropped into a shallow divot created by the tree fall. I momentarily lost my balance, but the weight and momentum of the bergen on my back pulled me awkwardly to the left. As I fell, my foot remained trapped divot. I heard a distinct "pop" as my knee gave way and white pain shot through my leg. I tried not to curse out loud. Kev, who was beside me, dropped his bergen on the ground to help pull me up. I staggered to my feet. I felt an immediate and building sense of dread but reassured Kev that I was good to continue. No more than five minutes later, and having seen our pace slow dramatically, the DS shadowing our patrol called me to one side. "Edwards. Drop your bergen with the patrol and follow me."

Hobbling out of the tree line with the DS, I walked down a gravel track to the waiting green army ambulance. "Get in and see the doctor," were his orders. I hopped up the two metal steps on one leg and sat down on the bench next to the army medic. Trying not to grimace as he twisted and rotated my knee one way then the other, and despite my protests to the contrary, I soon found myself on the way to Penrith Hospital. All I wanted to do was to be back in the cold forest helping my team to dig an OP. I needed to finish what I had started, what I had come here to achieve, but the pain and swelling in my knee determined otherwise. At the hospital, I was told that I'd likely suffered an anterior cruciate ligament injury in the fall and had torn some of the fibres and ligaments in my knee. Returning to the undulating, frozen depths of the forest was not going to be an option. Once I'd been driven in the medic's wagon back to the barracks, I sat with my head in my hands utterly dejected, heartbroken, and disappointed. Everything I'd worked for now seemed out of reach.

Two days later, as I prepared to head back home, the Regimental Sergeant Major of 23SAS walked into the room. "Edwards, I'm sorry about what happened. Trust me, I wish we could've just sent you straight back out. But rest up, rehabilitate, and make sure you don't give up," came his kind, reassuring words.

"Third time lucky, is it?" I joked. He laughed, wished me well, and saw me to the waiting wagon. However this had ended, and regardless of the disappointment, I knew that I had a long road ahead of me to rebuild and come back stronger.

4

HITTING ROCK BOTTOM

The 6th of August 2016 was a beautifully warm, sunny day in North Wales. I was making the short journey from Shrewsbury, Shropshire to a well-known cliff face near Llangollen called World's End with my best friend and regular climbing partner, Matt. As we arrived at the base of the cliff, excited for the day ahead, I looked up at the soaring vertical rock face blissfully unaware of the twist of fate that lurked ahead of me. This would be the last time I'd stand here, beneath this rockface, as the man I was proud to be.

World's End towers above the surrounding valley. Emerging from the forest below, it is made up of three prominent cliffs, each more than 40ft in height, stacked enticingly on top of each other like jagged, grey pieces of Jenga. I'd not yet had the opportunity to climb the last of Llangollen's towering rockfaces, so today would see new ground broken in my evolving levels of climbing experience. Matt and I began our ascent across the loose, steep scree that led to the first section of the cliff. We talked almost exclusively about the first date that Matt was going on later that evening, and we joked about each other's dating history – as good friends often do. For me, it felt like life was heading in the right direction, perhaps for the first time. I was happy in a long-term relationship with my girlfriend Ellie, about to start my first job as a history teacher at a local secondary school, plans were beginning to take shape for an ascent of Everest in 2018, and I would soon restart my quest to pass continuation training with 23SAS. Life was filled with promise.

Taking the lead, I began to ascend the first vertical section of the rock face. As I moved up the first 40ft pitch, I unclipped the climbing nuts and cams hanging from my harness and inserted them into cracks and fissures in the rock, before pulling the rope up from beneath me and clipping it onto my harness. Moving with balance, control and fluidity, I ascended to a small, grassy ledge high above Matt, who was about 25ft below me belaying from the narrow ledge I'd left. It felt so good to be standing here. Connected to the rock. Connected to nature. This was my playground, my happy place.

We spent the best part of three hours crisscrossing the rockface that afternoon, looking up the various climbing routes available in my pocket guidebook, before selecting a final route of increased difficulty and severity. One more climb. Just one last ascent I persuaded and promised Matt, who by this stage was counting down the hours and minutes before he'd swap chalk-stained climbing shorts and a t-shirt for something more befitting of a first date. I found one more route, an enticing but challenging crack running vertically up the length of the cliff from where we were standing, perhaps no more than an inch wide to the top, 35ft above us and 90ft above the forest floor. After several false starts, working out how best to position my body, I began to work my way up, inserting nuts and cams into the fissure in the jagged white limestone that had been baked in the sun and was red-hot to touch, attaching the rope that connected Matt and I to each other and anchored us to the face. Glancing down quickly at Matt below me, I got a real sense of how exposed I was, and how sheer the cliff was leading down to its base over 100ft below.

With one last shift of body position, I pushed up onto the final ledge above me and mantled my way to the top. Standing at the top, now 35ft above Matt, I felt like I'd conquered the world. I exchanged a wry smile with Matt, puffed out my cheeks in exhaustion and set about setting up a position from which I could safely belay Matt as he climbed up to my position at the top of the cliff. Once I was in position, I gave Matt the signal to begin his climb. He started strongly, using the power in his upper body to get midway up the first section. However, the crux of the climb required you to shift your body from the right of the crack across to the left. After a couple of failed attempts, Matt decided to call it quits. With my climbing gear still hanging on the rockface between the two of us, we made the decision that I'd retrieve my gear and then abseil back down to Matt and the small ledge he was currently standing on.

No more than a couple of minutes later, I'd managed to rearrange the anchor point through which my rope would run and was ready to abseil. Balancing on a small section of the ledge, my heels hanging over the void, I looked over my shoulder one final time before committing myself to the descent. However, as I turned to look forward, it was as if someone had pulled my legs from beneath me. Suddenly, I felt a sinking feeling in the pit of my stomach as my body began to accelerate from beneath me. The section of rock I was standing on had broken away from the main face of the cliff and before I could react quickly enough it had collapsed beneath my feet. In that moment, and in the milli-seconds and seconds that followed, life seemed to move in slow motion.

As I began to fall backward, I grasped desperately at the climbing rope running through the carabiner on my harness.

I reacted too slowly. Paralysed by fear. All I could hear was the rope zipping at high speed through my carabiner, which emitted a high-pitched whizzing noise. My eyes struggled to focus as I tumbled uncontrollably down the rockface, one second looking toward the sky, the next watching the cliff rush past in a sickening blur. The two almost blended into one. I couldn't say exactly how long the fall lasted, but in my reality, it felt like an eternity. For the first time in my life, my entire existence was put into perspective. I could sense exactly what I was about to lose – my girlfriend Ellie, my incredible family, my amazing friends, and the promise of the future. Everything. It's a scary thought, coming to terms with the fact that you're about to die. You don't welcome it, yet you know that the logical conclusion to the events in motion ultimately ends the same way.

In desperation, I shouted Matt's name as loud as I could three times. I remember the fear in my voice was unmistakable. The only thing I could do was to warn him that I was hurtling back down towards him so that he would have time to move out of harm's way. In the last moments of the fall, I looked up at the clear blue sky above. A moment of tranquillity and peace before the impact. A second later, my body slammed violently onto the ledge where Matt had been standing. I landed flat on my back, breaking my spine on impact (although I wouldn't know this until later). My body carried so much momentum and speed that after hitting the ledge I continued tumbling uncontrollably toward the next vertical section of the rockface. My arms flailed out to the side, desperate to grab onto anything that could arrest my fall. Nothing worked. It all happened too quickly. Just as I gave up all hope, I felt a sudden, powerful impact that stopped my body dead in its tracks. Upon hearing my shouts of warning, Matt reacted just in time by sprinting from his position against the cliff and lunging forward, throwing his body on top of mine and pinning me against the ledge. He had just saved my life.

In those first few seconds after breaking my fall, and as he checked that I was both alive and conscious, my mind struggled to compute the speed and gravity of what had just happened. I was in a state of total shock. Then I became aware of my body. The first thing I could feel was a searing pain in my right arm, and I saw that the ledge beneath it was soaked with blood. A deep laceration ran from the middle of my forearm up to the top of my shoulder. With the pain growing stronger by the second, I responded by trying to stand up. As I pushed with my arms and shoulders, I felt as if the whole world had pivoted through the middle of my back. No matter how hard I tried, I couldn't move my legs. They simply stayed lifeless beneath me. My mind racing with panic after each failed attempt to pick myself up from the dirt, a growing realisation spread through me that surviving this fall had potentially come at a significant cost. I couldn't feel or move anything below my chest.

Matt jumped into action, shouting to the climbers I had seen earlier on a route nearby for help, before calling 999 and requesting the support of the local Mountain Rescue team. Staring up at the sky, I could hear and see the commotion happening around me but was still totally unable to move or help myself. As the adrenaline that had been pumping through my body began to wear off, and as the pain from my back reached a level I'd never experienced, I began to get some sense of how badly injured I was. Matt relayed to me that the Mountain Rescue team and HM Coastguard had been informed and were responding. They'd be at least 30 minutes to our location. Matt did his best to keep me talking, to distract me from passing out from the pain. Call it delirium, or perhaps even stupidity, but it was as we waited for the Coastguard helicopter to appear on the horizon, that I made the most important commitment of my life. No matter what came next, I would never give up or be beaten by what had just happened. I had to do this for my family, for my friends, but most importantly, for myself.

Just as the Coastguard chopper began to hover above World's End, the initial contingent of the local Mountain Rescue team arrived on the scene, led by Dave, the team's doctor. He introduced himself and asked me to rate my pain score out of 10. I lied through my teeth and said, "Seven". He paused, then laughed, and told me that they had just rescued someone with a broken finger who had said nine. In my mind, he was giving me permission to admit my vulnerability. When he asked for a second time, I replied accurately, "It's a bloody solid 10". Dave administered the first dose of morphine, which instantly took the edge off my pain. I could feel the powerful downblast of the HM Coastguard helicopter hovering high above the cliff as it lowered its winchman down to assist the Mountain Rescue team in formulating an evacuation plan. The team busied themselves around me, stabilising the situation by moving me across to a spinal board. It was at this point, so close to being evacuated from this living hell, that I watched the Coastguard helicopter fly off into the distance. In my confused state, I tried to reach up as if to try and grab the helicopter to stop it from disappearing into the distance. The helicopter's winchman, who had stayed with me, calmed me down and reassured me that it would be back once it had refuelled.

Flat on my back, surrounded by unfamiliar faces, and totally out of control for the first time in my life, it felt like an eternity before the faint drone of the returning helicopter came into earshot. The torturous wait for evacuation was coming to an end, close to three hours after the rescue teams had arrived. As the helicopter hovered perilously close to the cliff above, the team on the ground moved me from the plastic spinal board onto a cocooned spinal board that inflated around my body, rendering me motionless. I remember Matt came over at that point and leant over me, shielding me from the downdraft of the helicopter above. We said an emotional goodbye, and seconds later I was airborne, being winched up towards the open flight door of the Merlin helicopter above.

The journey starts here…

5

A DIARY FOR THE JOURNEY AHEAD

Aboard the HM Coastguard Merlin helicopter en route to the nearest Major Trauma Unit, I struggled to remain conscious despite the best efforts of Steve, the crew's winchman. In my morphine-induced haze, coupled with the thumping, rhythmic vibration of the rotor blades above, the flight to Royal Stoke University Hospital seemed to last no more than a few minutes. Touch down. Steve's face appeared for the last time; he grabbed my hand and said, "Good luck mate," as he helped cross-load me from the helicopter onto the waiting hospital stretcher. The air cocoon I'd been lifted from the cliffside in was replaced with a yellow spinal board and head brace, and I was rushed across the landing pad and into Accident & Emergency.

The bright fluorescent lights of the hospital blurred into a single line as I was rushed through various hallways and corridors. Unable to move my head, I relied on my peripheral vision to discern what was going on, who the strangers were surrounding me, and what they were saying. It was a losing battle. Exhaustion, fatigue, and morphine washed over me in waves of oblivion. One moment, I'd be perfectly lucid as the medical team cut away my dirt- and blood-stained clothing, talking to them as if I were catching up with old friends, the next, unable to keep my eyes open any longer, my reality faded to black. The grave nature of my injury didn't truly dawn on me until I found myself lying inside a doughnut-shaped MRI scanner for the first time. Engulfed by the beeping, clicking, thudding, and whirring noises of the scanner, my mind drifted to what could be the worst-case scenario result. I was so incredibly scared, but I knew that I had to stay mentally strong. It was all I had left.

My worst fears were confirmed later that evening when "Doctor Ed" told me that I had sustained a "significant injury" to my spine, and to the spinal cord itself. It was the word "significant" that replayed in my mind like a broken record. I asked Ed the question I most feared the answer to, but I needed to know. "Will I ever walk again?" I asked, trying to mask the desperation in my voice.

Ed responded without hesitation, "Darren, this is a significant injury". He didn't need to say it for me to put two and two together. I hadn't been able to feel or move below my chest, no matter how hard I tried, for more than five hours by this point. It was the first time I felt vulnerable.

As I waited for the arrival of the hospital's leading neurosurgeon, who had answered the call to perform my surgery despite being on annual leave at the time, I regained consciousness in time to see my Mum's face appear, followed by my Dad's. I felt so relieved to see them, yet so guilty at the same time for having put them through what they must have always feared about my climbing. "I'm so sorry Mum," was the first thing I said as I reached my hand out toward hers. I wanted to be her little boy again, to be told that everything would be all right – which is exactly what she said. Moments later, I saw Ellie rushing across the hospital bay toward me, her eyes already noticeably teary as she softly embraced me as best she could.

I struggled to see her so emotional, particularly as there was nothing I could do to make the situation better or to make up for what I was putting her through. I fell asleep holding her hand. The next time I would see her was after my surgery.

In the early hours of 7 August 2016, I underwent a complex and lengthy surgery to stabilise my spine. Both my X-ray and MRI scans revealed that I had snapped my back into two separate pieces around chest level, such was the force of the impact when I fell. There was considerable damage to my spinal cord, and little hope that anything would be salvageable. Of lesser concern, but also mentioned, was that I'd broken several of the ribs next to the break in my spine, which had resulted in a partially collapsed lung known as a pneumothorax. The surgery lasted roughly eight hours. God knows how my family, Ellie, Matt, and everyone waiting for me to come out during those long hours.

Darkness surrounded me. I forced my eyelids to open. The bright haze of fluorescent lighting dazzled my vision. "Where am I?", "Why can't I move?" I thought out loud to anyone who would listen, utterly confused about where I was, and why I couldn't move my legs. In those first bleary-eyed moments of awareness, I had forgotten that I was in a hospital. Before I could get the attention of the nurse walking past the foot of my bed, I slipped back into darkness. The next time I regained consciousness, I saw the faces of my surgeon and anaesthetist standing at the foot of my bed. Everything started to click back in place. The surgeon began speaking; his tone was calm and friendly but the news wasn't positive or welcoming. Over the course of the next few minutes, I listened in a dream-like state as he revealed the severity of my injury and the stark truth of his prognosis for any future recovery. Whilst my surgery had been complex, the team had managed to successfully reconnect the snapped T6/T7 vertebrae with the use of two 10-inch titanium rods, now screwed into place along the length of my spine. However, the operation also revealed extensive and significant damage to my spinal cord – there was that word again: "significant". In my moment of greatest darkness, I committed myself to optimism, to never giving up, and to the hope that my condition might improve in the coming days and weeks.

The next five days were spent in a morphine-induced haze in the hospital's Intensive Care Unit. The ICU was like nothing I'd ever experienced before. The rhythmic beeping of machines at my bedside, the screams of other patients in pain, the constant movement of staff across the ward, the harsh fluorescent lighting. With my body's circadian rhythm out of kilter, and no discernible pattern by which the ward abided, I'd completely lost any sense of either time or date. In those moments of confusion, I found familiarity and strength in those who stood beside me. There was a core group who never seemed to be far away: Matt, Ellie, Mum and my sister Eve. Our conversations may have been limited by how long I could stay lucid, but they each had their way of being the emotional crutch I needed in those dark moments. Matt helped me to reflect on what had happened, filling in the blanks for me from his experience that day, but already casting an eye to the future and looking forward to our "next epic adventure together".

At some point in that first week in the ICU, Ellie sat next to me and produced a leather diary. "A diary for the journey ahead," she said with determined enthusiasm. For the next few days, she would sit next to me and summarise each day on my behalf and then ask for a contribution from me. I managed two words that first day: "dry" (my body was constantly overheating because of the surgery, and it was a battle to stay hydrated) and "positive". The next day, the only contribution I could manage was "sleepy". As the days passed, I felt a growing sense of suffocation about life in the ICU. I struggled with the lack of control I could exert on my own body, let alone my own life. As much as I tried, my condition hadn't improved. I didn't know it at the time, but on the fourth day, Ellie sat beside me and wrote in my diary: "I hate to put words in your mouth, but I think you are finding everything a little hard today". She had hit the nail on the head, although I tried my best not to show it.

One thing that was helping to keep me mentally strong, even amongst the seemingly catastrophic wreckage of "life" at that precise moment, was a clear sense of perspective – of how lucky I'd been. In the seconds after I had plummeted from that ledge, and the seconds before Matt brought my uncontrolled tumble to a halt, I'd achieved an unparalleled sense of clarity as to how bloody precious life, and those within it, is. When I looked at my situation through that lens, even in my barely lucid state in ICU, each additional second on this Earth seemed like a gift. How lucky I was to have people in my corner, like my Mum, who somehow convinced two of the nurses to push me and my bed (machines and all) out of the ICU and into an area below the hospital's ambulance loading bay – just so that I could feel the sun on my face and the cool breeze against my skin for the first time in five days. When I teetered dangerously close to feeling emotionally overwhelmed, it was moments like this, and the actions of those closest to me, that pulled me through.

With each day that passed my body grew stronger, and my reliance upon intravenous morphine decreased, but my neurological condition remained unchanged. I would muster enough energy to pull the sheets up from the bottom of my bed to expose my feet, and then proceed to do rep after rep to send a signal down to my big toe (or any toe for that matter), in the hope of even the faintest flicker of movement. As I began to approach the week anniversary of my accident, it was decided that I was stable enough to be transferred across to the Midland Centre for Spinal Injuries, where I would begin the next stage of my recovery before starting physical rehabilitation. On the day of my transfer, I felt a great sense of pride; I'd graduated to the next stage of my recovery, putting further distance between the vivid memory of my accident and my future. As I was wheeled out of the ICU on a spinal board for the last time, I had a chance to say goodbye to Maryanne, the nurse who had first tended to my wounds and prepped me for surgery. "Remember what you said – never give in!" were her last words to me as I was pushed toward the exit.

6

DREAMING OF TOMORROW

The first, and perhaps most crucial, part of the rehabilitation process following serious spinal cord injury is six weeks of enforced bed rest. By strictly limiting movement in the spine, the body can better utilise its resources to promote growth and repair the damaged area. Whilst the thought of lying flat on my back 24 hours a day for the next six weeks was a bitter pill to swallow, the knowledge that some patients had seen either partial or near-full recovery within this timeframe gave me hope that I might be one of those special few. However, it was that same promise of hope that made each day a desperate search for any sign of change or improvement in my condition.

In a slice of good fortune, it turned out that the Midland Centre for Spinal Injuries was, to my surprise, located just 30 minutes from my hometown of Shrewsbury. Once I'd been wheeled through yet another maze of corridors and side-exits, made even more disorienting given the fact all I could see was the ceiling and the fleeting sight of an overhead sign, I was taken into what would be my very own room – my very own room! After the constant hustle and bustle of life in the ICU, I was struck by the comparative peace and tranquillity of my new surroundings. It felt like I had space to breathe, and a safe environment from which to start the process of recovering physically and emotionally.

The staff at MCSI made it their business to make me feel as welcomed as possible on my first day on the ward, taking turns to pop their head through the door and introduce themselves. In a unit where the average length of stay for most patients would be roughly four months, it was no surprise that the word "family" kept being used to describe the relationship between patient and staff. Of all the team I met that first afternoon in MCSI, it as a Health Care Assistant, who went by the nickname Rocky, who would leave a lasting and positive impact on my stay. When she first introduced herself, she joked that they called her Rocky because she was "hard as nails" whilst putting up her fists and beginning to shadow box around my room like Rocky Balboa. She succeeded in putting a smile on my face, an effect she'd have every time she entered my room from that moment on. And, as I'd already figured out from watching her boxing, she was a teddy bear at heart.

Unlike my experience in the ICU, my life would now be dictated by an easy-to-follow pattern to each day: 07:00 would be my morning wake-up (not my choice to have it that early), breakfast at 08:00, "bed physio" at 10:00, lunch at 12:30, dinner at 18:00 and finally lights out at 22:00. Time would also be factored into each day for the medically critical procedures required to keep me in good health now that I was living with a Spinal Cord Injury, primarily: managing my bladder, bowels, and daily washing. The only problem was that the majority of these procedures involved the most intimate areas of my body, and there seemed to be an abundance of young, attractive, female members of staff who were a regular feature of this daily knock to my dignity and pride. There were even moments where I had to resist the temptation to say, "It usually looks bigger, I promise," as they were mid-way through inserting a catheter into my penis.

In between all this "fun and games" would be time for the things that would help to get me through the next five weeks – visits from family and friends. The fact that MCSI was so close to home meant that there was an almost constant flow of visits, which helped to generate positive energy about life in my otherwise solitary room. Whilst the ward operated a rule of two visitors per patient at any one time, my small room often became a social hub with five, six, seven (or more) piling in at any one time. The frequent offenders included Ellie, my family, Matt, and Matt's family, which could quickly escalate to a total of nine people trying to keep a low profile as they huddled around my bed. In moments like this, there was no shortage of positive morale pumping across the room, helping to keep me focused and strong. There was no mournful, nostalgic reminiscing of what had been lost, or how life would never be the same, only an embracing of how a positive mindset would enable me to bounce back stronger than ever before and defy all expectations.

• • •

My eyes fluttered slowly open as I woke from another deep sleep. I stretched out my arms above me, tensed my legs, and wiggled my toes as I fought the temptation to fall back to sleep. *Oh my God*. I can feel my legs. Bloody hell, I can move my bloody toes! In a moment of pure, vivid elation, I tilted my face toward the door and began to shout, "Nurse! Somebody, please come quickly!" Nothing short of a miracle had happened overnight. But, as I shouted with every ounce of conviction possible, I began to feel an overwhelming urge to fall back asleep, total exhaustion blanketed me. I drifted inexorably back to sleep. Moments later, I woke with a sense of dread; a glance across the room confirmed that no one had responded to my call. I still needed to share my news. Yet, as I looked down at my body, I knew that I didn't feel the same as I had only moments before. I couldn't feel my legs. I couldn't wiggle my toes. But it had all felt so real, so vivid. "It's fucking happened again," I said out loud, in anguish. I'd been here before. Felt this heart-breaking disappointment before. This was the fifth night in a row I'd had this exact, cruel dream. It all felt so real.

Three weeks had passed since my life changed. I continued my daily battle to stay mentally positive and to search for any glimpse of improvement in my condition. None had come. My recurring morning dream was the closest I had got to escaping the paralysis that besieged my body. As the days and weeks drifted on, it seemed to me that everyone's lives were carrying on as normal – except for my own. Staring out of my doorway through to the room opposite, I watched with growing envy as Steve, a patient who had been admitted to the ward at a similar time to me, began to feel and move his legs for the first time since his injury. I'd never truly experienced envy before. I'd never been envious of someone else's life or their achievements, certainly not enough to feel the mixture of anger, jealousy and inferiority that consumed me now. I didn't know Steve, but I was happy for him. With each day his condition improved further, and I could sense that he would be one of the lucky ones – a group I longed to be part of.

There were so many aspects to my present existence that I had no control over, but I learnt to relinquish that control and play the long game, knowing that eventually I would regain control of my life. Nevertheless, I had become so wrapped up in trying to force my body to do things that it *couldn't* control that

I was growing increasingly frustrated. I felt almost betrayed by the lack of neurological improvement, despite my huge efforts. I knew I needed to switch up my mindset. Fortunately, as I approach the halfway mark of my time on bed rest, I was presented with two opportunities that enabled me to do this.

One morning, one of the hospital's physios, Amy, came into my room with a gift, proudly presenting me with something she called a spirometer. "It looks like a child's toy," I remarked, laughing at the thought of the plastic tubes and ping pong balls in front of me being a legitimate medical training device.

"It does look a bit like a Victorian Christmas present, doesn't it?" she joked back. "In all seriousness though, it's designed to test your lung function, and will show us how your lungs have healed since the one collapsed."

A plastic breathing tube led to three chambers, each containing a single ping pong ball. A healthy adult could, with a regular inhale, lift all three balls to the top of their respective chambers. Eager to prove my cardiovascular prowess, I took the spirometer from Amy, placed the plastic tube to my lips and inhaled with all my might. I barely wobbled the first ping pong ball. I was speechless (and clearly breathless as well). It was the first real indication of how weak my body was. Amy placed the spirometer on my bedside table and told me to practice at least once a day. She had unwittingly placed a red flag in front of a bull. From that moment on, and in every spare moment I had in that room (there were a lot), I gave my all to lifting that first ball to the top of its chamber. Then I focused on wobbling the second ball, and so on. This small lump of plastic became a focal point for my physical recovery. It was exactly the intervention I'd needed, at just the right time.

As days continued to tick by at a predictably pedestrian pace, I became increasingly aware of how others were responding emotionally to my injury. Those closest to me – my friends, family, the guys I'd gone through SAS Reserve selection with – knew me well enough to know that I'd never quit. They knew that I'd stay true to the promise I made to myself on that cliffside. In many respects, it was those who knew me from looser circumstances who struggled to see me marooned on a hospital bed, unable to do many of the things they'd associated me with as a person. There was a funny irony about moments like this, when I'd find myself consoling the person who had come to visit me, reassuring them, "Don't worry, I'll be okay, I promise," as they mentally catastrophised the helpless nature of the situation. Weirdly, visits like this spurred me on; they kept me true to my word – strong in mind, if not in body.

Of all the potential insecurities and worries about my future, my main fear was losing Ellie. She was my emotional crutch, the face that with just one smile could lift my mood, the hope for a future full of love and adventure. "I think we'll be one of those couples that people will look at and admire, almost in amazement at how strong we are together," I said one afternoon.

She looked at me, tucked her long brown hair behind her ears, and replied, "As soon as you're better, we'll go running in the hills together again. You just need to focus on getting better first." I smiled, the thought of us defying the odds together a vivid figment of my imagination. It was something to aim for, something worth fighting for.

"Do you love me unconditionally, Ellie?" I asked, a clear hint of insecurity in my voice.

"Of course, Darren" she replied in an oddly impersonal tone. "Remember, you've got your six-week review with Doctor Osman next week; it'll be interesting to see your scans and to see what his prognosis is for your recovery," she continued. I nodded my head in agreement. We both wanted there to be some good news next week and for my latest set of scans to show some positive progress.

That week passed slowly, save for the distraction of visits and coverage of the 2016 Rio Olympics on the tiny TV above my bed. Even though I'd always enjoyed watching athletes at the peak of their physical prowess, it did at times make difficult viewing emotionally – I'd always prided myself on being highly fit and active. Finally, it was time for my six-week review. As my bed was being pushed down the corridor to an adjoining consultation room, Ellie followed closely behind with a notebook and pen in her hand and an anxious expression across her face. Doctor Osman was sitting in the corner of the room, a projector already beaming a set of images onto the white wall behind him. He introduced the set of scans as the X-rays and MRIs taken on the day of my injury. "As you can see, there was extensive damage to the spinal column, resulting in a total dislocation of your spine at T6. Your MRI evidences a significant volume of damage to the spinal cord itself – perhaps as bad as you can get without severing the cord entirely." I'd already prepared myself mentally to hear the hard truths of my injury, that wasn't my concern, my thought process was entirely focused on the potential for future recovery.

Looking directly at Doctor Osman, I asked impatiently, "I get that the damage was initially severe, but what about my chances of regaining any function below the level of my injury…what are my chances of walking again?"

I paid close attention to his expression. He immediately broke eye contact with me, furrowing his brow as he began to answer, his gaze still avoiding my own. "Mr Edwards, I'm afraid that based on all the cases like your own that I've seen on this ward, it is my assessment that your condition is permanent. As for walking, I'm incredibly sorry..."

His words sliced into me. The concise, clinical answer I'd long feared had been verbalised, made real. Ellie jumped to my defence, but her words and Doctor Osman's were now just background noise as I retreated into my mind, desperately trying to recalibrate the images and beliefs I'd once held about my future life. A pang of uncertainty hit me, unearthing perhaps my greatest fear...what would this mean for my future with Ellie?

7

TAKING BACK CONTROL

For the last six weeks, the staff at MCSI had counted down each week and each day with me as I got closer to the triumphant landmark that would see me leave a hospital bed for the first time since the day my life changed. I had watched helplessly as my muscle mass slowly deserted my body, unable to take pride in my physical strength as I once had. But today marked the day that I would start to take back control of my life.

I woke that morning, as I had every other for the last four weeks, my painfully vivid dream duping me for a moment that I could feel and move my legs again. But this morning was different to all those that had preceded it. Nicky, one of the most charismatic nurses on the ward, burst energetically into the room and declared, "Today's the day, Darren!" with a beaming smile across her face. I raised my fist triumphantly into the air, adrenaline pumping through my veins at the thought of escaping the confines of this bed, if only for 30 minutes – as was common practice on the first day. If I exceeded 30 minutes, there was every chance I would pass out, my body having grown too weak to pump blood vertically.

It was midday by the time the electric hoist was brought into my room. Nicky and Sarah dressed me before carefully placing a harness underneath my body. The hoist tightened around me, raising me into a sitting position before slowly lifting my body inch by inch from what had been my home for the last six weeks. The excitement I felt at that moment was immeasurable. But, as the hoist lifted me higher, I looked down to see a pair of thin, lifeless legs swinging limply beneath me. It didn't strike me right away...they were my legs. For the first time since the day of my accident, I got a true sense of the extent of my injury, and of how alien parts of my body looked and felt to me. As I lifted my head, I noticed that Nicky and Sarah were both smiling broadly at me, full of joy to be sharing this moment with me. I tried my best to smile through the pain and to put on a brave face, but on the inside I was hurting. Sitting in a wheelchair for the first time in my life, I wanted nothing more than to return to the safety of the very thing I'd craved escaping for the last six weeks – my bed. I felt overwhelmed by a sense of loss for the first time.

As I lay in bed that night, I thought back to the emotional torment of the day. I *had* to reframe how I felt about everything. I couldn't allow these feelings of doubt and fear to consume me. From that moment on, I committed myself to improving my situation each day, regardless of how incrementally small that may appear to the outside world. I had to finish each day mentally and physically stronger than I started it. There were always going to be events and obstacles that would push me to the edge; I had to accept that and not allow it to derail my recovery journey. It was a defining moment for me.

The next morning, I woke with a fierce determination to hold onto that commitment and reframe the helplessness and fear I had felt the day before. The nursing team came in at mid-morning with the hoist and harness ready. Matt arrived just in time to be there to support me. I'd confided in him the night before about my moment of weakness. Unlike yesterday, I knew what to expect now. I had mentally primed myself for how things were going to look and feel. One key difference would be that I'd have Matt by my side, an omnipresent source of strength since the day he saved my life. As I was lowered into the archaic-looking electric wheelchair at the side of my bed, I looked up at Matt and managed a genuine, warm smile. I felt exactly how I'd expected to feel this time yesterday – eager to seize every ounce of independence I could. Matt smiled at me, pointed toward the door, and with a wry smile, said, "Ready for an adventure?" For the next 30 minutes, we embarked on a grand expedition across hospital grounds – explorers of the world once again!

For the first six weeks of my rehabilitation programme, I had to use the electric wheelchair as the metalwork in my spine was still too fragile to risk pushing (or falling out of) a manual chair. Whilst it was a relic of the 1980s (and far too slow for my liking), it became my ticket to freedom and an independence I hadn't experienced in so long. Visits from friends and family would of course continue, but I now had a busy timetable of physiotherapy, occupational therapy, and patient education seminars to attend. This is where I started to take back control.

• • •

It was Monday morning, time for my first rehabilitation session. I'd been delighted to learn that Amy would be my dedicated physio, whom I'd built a good bond with since my first weeks on the ward. We headed across the room to one of the physio plinths, and she explained that we were going to start by working on my sitting balance; sounds easy, right?

After being hoisted from my chair to the edge of the plinth, Amy and another physio worked together to prop me up. Even with their hands firmly holding me in place, I felt unsteady. Amy carefully manoeuvred herself in front of me, looked me in the eyes and said, "Ready to try and keep your balance?"

I smiled nervously but answered with a confident, "Let's do this!"

As soon as the pair relaxed their grip, I lurched uncontrollably backwards onto a pile of pillows placed behind me for exactly this reason. On my second attempt, I almost headbutted Amy as I fell forward. Paralysed from the chest down, I could no longer control the muscles in my core, hips, or legs – pretty much all your essentials for balancing effectively. Again and again, I kept trying, kept failing, but never lost the determination to improve, even fractionally, with each attempt. Here was the first challenge that I had to rise to – or to "sit to", I should say!

Occupational Therapy under the guidance of Paula, was about implementing the skills I'd be learning with Amy into practice in the real world – like getting in and out of a car, into a bath,] or transferring across to a toilet. All these things sounded, dare I say it, easy to start with – until we started practising. Desperate to show how hard I was willing to work to improve, I'd routinely find myself in the gap between my chair and the car, or my chair and the toilet, not yet having the upper body strength and balance required to prevent each transfer from turning into an amusing spectacle. It didn't take many sessions together before Paula looked at me, and said with a humorous tint to her voice, "You're in trouble, aren't you?" as she picked me up from the floor between my chair and a toilet seat. She wasn't wrong.

With increased, albeit modest, levels of freedom and an ability to roam across the hospital, I started to forge genuine bonds with the other patients at MCSI. One of these patients was Tim, who on his way cycling to work one day was hit by a lorry driver on his mobile phone, instantly and irreversibly changing the course of Tim's life in a flash. Like me, Tim had been incredibly lucky to survive – although he assured me that the lorry had come off worse in the collision. That pretty much summed Tim up: he had a great ability to contextualise everything with humour and was a significantly positive influence as I began my rehabilitation. He was a couple of weeks ahead of me on his journey, so whilst I struggled to learn the art of sitting balance, from across the room I'd see Tim working on more physically demanding lifts and movements. He inspired me.

The weeks continued to tick by, and in their own slow hospital time-warp kind of way, I held to my commitment to start each day mentally and physically stronger than I had the day before. I'd made great progress in my sessions with Amy and Paula, although falling over was still a routine feature as we increased the intensity and frequency of the lifts, moves and balancing. Amy and I had formed a great dynamic in our sessions, with humour a core pillar of anything and everything we did, but she also knew that I liked to be constantly challenged. Enlisting the help of one of the ward's Physio Assistants, Kate, who introduced herself to me as "the Sergeant Major", I paid my way in sweat whenever the two teamed up to deliver a brutal session. Kate's go-to phrase was always, "Suck it up, princess."

I was approaching the final weekend of what had been six long weeks of extra restrictions when I hadn't been allowed to use a manual wheelchair, when I was given the rare and priceless opportunity to leave the hospital for the day. For 12 weeks, I had seen nothing but the clinical interior of hospital buildings, surrounded by beeping machines and the smell of chemical cleaning products. Ellie had grand plans afoot for my first day away from the hospital, which remained a mystery until I began to recognise our direction of travel as we drove south from MCSI – we were headed for the Shropshire hills! As we ascended the single-track road leading to the top of Cardingmill Valley, I began to reconnect with this world that had been lost to me for so long, its vibrant natural colours, lush woodland, and beautifully undulating landscape. I'd not seen such beauty since the day my world changed. We spent close to three hours venturing across the top of the valley, working as a team to get over the bumpy ground, laughing to ourselves as we contemplated the reaction of the hospital staff to this overly audacious escape (Ellie had told them we were going to a garden centre). Rattling along the gravel track in my clunky NHS wheelchair, I was as happy as could be. For the first time since my injury, I felt a quiet sense of contentment and confidence for our future together.

8

CRASH LAND

"Come on Darren, push! You can do this!" Amy yelled as I tried with all my might to lift myself out of my wheelchair. I tightly gripped the wooden frame in front of me, my arms trembling underneath my weight as I tried to lift myself into a standing position. "You're doing great Darren. Come on, keep pushing yourself up," roared Amy. With one big final effort, I extended my triceps to their full extent and rose to being 6ft tall for the first time in three months. "STOP! STOP! STOP!" came a desperate plea from Amy suddenly. In a panic, I glanced down, and noticed that I'd pushed so hard that I'd lifted my feet clean off the floor! Lowering myself back down, Amy and Ruth (another fantastic physio on the ward) strapped a belt around my hips and secured me into the wooden standing frame.

The feeling was unreal. There I was, standing back up again. Tall and proud. I couldn't have wiped the beaming smile from my face even if you'd paid me to. It was an incredibly special and poignant moment in my recovery journey – that was, until I fainted. I regained consciousness lying on a physio plinth with my legs held above me by Amy and Ruth, blood slowly flowing back to my brain. All we could do was laugh. It had been one hell of a re-introduction to standing – and certainly would not be the last.

Waving goodbye to my trusty electric wheelchair, upon which I had explored every nook and cranny of the hospital grounds (at incredibly slow speeds), it was time to start using a manual chair. My rehabilitation could now properly commence. I had graduated to the big league and Amy and the "Sergeant Major" (Kate) could now properly ramp up the intensity of my sessions. Kate looked particularly fired up about the prospect of teaching me how to use a manual wheelchair and joked somewhat seriously that "we'll have you bumping backwards downstairs in no time" with a fiendish look in her eyes. Now the risk of further complications because of the metal rods in my back my had been removed, the bar for progression would get steadily higher and higher before I'd be signed off and discharged from the hospital.

With my rehab schedule getting continually busier during the day, visits from friends and family tended to revolve around the evenings, which often brought the added benefit of a takeaway from the local Indian restaurant or KFC. Friendships also blossomed in the ward. Along with Tim, I was moved into a bay with two other patients named John and Michael. John was a father of two who woke up one morning paralysed from the waist down. A blood vessel had burst in his spine as he slept, changing the course of his life in an instant. It turned out that Michael was a monk – a proper kind of monk (just as you'd imagine). When the monastery's cat had got itself stranded on the roof of a third-storey building, Michael volunteered to mount a rescue mission. Up on the roof, he slipped on a wet tile and fell to the courtyard below, breaking his back on impact. (The cat was fine by the way.) The bond between the four of us grew strong incredibly quickly, perhaps because we were bound by shared experience, but also because our attitudes toward rehabilitation aligned in the sense that we had committed ourselves to making the most of our respective conditions.

Home was now within reach. If I could work hard over the next six weeks and prove that I could master all the elements necessary to live a thriving and independent life, I'd get to go home – a place I'd yearned for in the dark moments. But first I had to prove to Amy, Paula and the medical staff that I was ready to be discharged. I'd already started to take charge of managing my bladder and bowels, which meant using a catheter every four hours to go for a wee and transferring safely to a toilet with a rubber glove at the ready to help my body "drop the kids off at the pool" (we needn't say anymore). There are some elements to a Spinal Cord Injury where it is obvious to see what the challenges might be; having to use a wheelchair is an obvious example. But it's things like effectively managing bladder, bowels, medication, pain – those things you can't see – that are the hardest to negotiate without issue.

"Suck it up princess," Kate roared in front of me. "That was good. So, let's do it again," she continued. I looked up at her, sweat dripping from my brow, my heart beating out of my chest. There was no point protesting and I knew that I'd never admit to being spent physically. There was always one more go in me. We were practising getting off the floor and back into my wheelchair without the use of any aids or steps, using pure upper body strength alone. I'd been building up my strength through the weeks of physio and OT, as well as volunteering for extra strength and conditioning sessions in the gym. Kate certainly knew how to crack the proverbial whip and would simply make our sessions tougher the stronger I became. She often quipped, "It'll be worth it when you win that Gold medal at the Paralympics," as extra motivation. She was already touting me for a future in the Paralympics and

I'd only just learnt to lift myself off the floor and back into my chair, but I shared her ambition and optimism for the future!

It had been a busy period for Ellie, who was in her first year as a junior doctor at a local hospital. She'd been under a lot of pressure and had been working long shifts at awkward times concerning visiting hours at MCSI. We were seeing less of each other than at any time since my injury, which I understood and supported – I knew how hard she'd worked to qualify as a doctor and I didn't want to be a bigger source of pressure than I already was. When we did get to see each other, however, I felt a sense of disconnect that I hadn't experienced before. She seemed distant, her body language colder and more insular than normal. It was evident that she was struggling with the stresses and strains of her new career. It never occurred to me that there was an underlying issue below the surface, yet to appear. It was common knowledge across the ward that I wanted to propose to Ellie, who had been there for me since day one; I was just waiting until I was discharged to "pop the question".

It was a quiet afternoon, and I was enjoying the rarity of being the only one in the bay as I read my book. In the corner of my eye, I noticed someone walk into the bay…it was Ellie! My heart leapt. She hadn't said that she was coming to visit today. What an unexpected surprise. "Hello beautiful," I said as I leaned forward to give her a big hug. She embraced me, but it felt somewhat awkward. As she sat down on the chair next to my bed, I could see that she looked severely worried. She didn't look like the girl I knew. "Is everything okay Ellie?" I asked, concern evident in my voice. She looked at me, but then broke eye contact and stared at her lap as she responded.

"Darren. I came here to tell you that I can't do this anymore." Her voice was nervous and unsure.

With my mind full of confusion as to the real cause of her

angst, I responded, "Sorry El, what do you mean you can't do this anymore? Is it work?"

She looked up at me for the briefest of seconds, made eye contact, then looked back down at her lap. "Us. I'm so sorry Darren but I can't do *us* anymore. I can't be the one to help you through this. I just can't do it. I'm so sorry."

It felt like someone had driven a dagger into my heart. I tried to respond but could barely speak. I tripped over my words, desperate to say something, anything that would rectify the situation. Before I could respond, Ellie burst into tears in front of me. As I reached out to hold her, she stood up and said, "I'm so sorry Darren," before stumbling away from me and walking out of the ward.

I called out her name in desperation. She turned to look at me. "I love you!" They were the only words I thought I could say to change her mind.

Fighting back tears, her voice breaking, Ellie's last words to me were, "I'm so sorry," before she fled. My heart broke into a million pieces, spilling out onto the floor in front of me. It was the last time I'd ever see her.

I'd drawn such strength, safety and comfort from our relationship. Now, as it shattered in front of my eyes, I felt desperate, scared and suddenly very alone. The life I'd imagined for myself, for us, once I'd left the hospital was now nothing more than fantasy. For four months I had fought back against the emotion and pain of my injury, never once breaking down in tears, never letting the situation defeat me, until now. There was no defiance left. All I could do to process what had just happened was to cry, fumbling for my phone as I tried time and time again to call her mobile, desperate to plead with her not to leave me. My mind plagued me with memories of when we first met, memories of our happiest moments together

– why was I torturing myself like this? My worst fears had been realised. All along I'd feared that she might leave me, which was one of the reasons I'd stayed so strong in front of her, but that amounted to nothing now. There was nothing left. I felt no loss of dignity or pride as I broke down uncontrollably in the middle of my bay, tears pouring from my eyes, hyperventilating, panicking. I wanted the world to swallow me whole.

The end of our relationship marked the start of a daily battle for self-esteem, positivity, and any remnants of resilience I could find. I tried my best to mask my pain to everyone on the ward, although word had spread fast amongst the staff. I overheard a conversation between two nurses the next day as one of them exclaimed in shock, "She did what?!" and the other responded, "Yeah, I think it's been pretty devastating for Darren, bless him." Unfortunately, Amy bore the brunt of my hurt at our next physio session. I struggled to focus and kept messing up what we were doing. In my frustration I threw one of the softballs we were using across the room, my anger overflowing. Amy looked me in the eyes, full of sympathy, and said, "Darren, what do we do when life gives us lemons?" to which I simply replied, "Fuck lemons."

Each night I would pull the curtains around my bedspace, crawl into bed, put on my headphones and sob quietly in the hope that Tim, John, and Michael couldn't hear me. I'd listen to the lyrics of one song in particular, *Crash Land* by Twin Atlantic:

Because I'm stuck here on this island
And I've lost it all over again
Nothing gets better than memories
When all you have are memories of friends
I went searching when the lights went out
I went searching when my flight went down

9

FROM THE ZOO TO THE JUNGLE

There are times in life when we experience considerable adversity, in whichever form it might take, and there is no one right thing that people can say to effectively console us. This was one of those moments. No matter the logically sound perspectives my family, friends, or hospital staff brought to me, I wasn't ready to hear them. I didn't want to hear "It'll get easier with each day that passes, Darren." That seemed an utterly stupid concept to someone battling with raw, uncontrollable emotions – one minute denial, the next frustration and anger. I saw my original discharge date come and go. Now that I had nowhere to be discharged to, life seemed helpless and pointless. How could anyone ever love me like this when the one person I thought loved me unconditionally couldn't? I sat out on the hospital's helicopter pad in the middle of a cold December downpour and realised that I didn't know how to pull myself from the wreckage this time.

"Darren, what on earth are you doing out here?" came a voice from behind me. I turned to see Kate striding across the tarmac. "You're utterly soaked! Come on, let's get you back inside and changed," she continued as she put her arm around my shoulders and started to lead us back to the main hospital building. Once I'd had a warm shower and put on some dry clothes, Kate came into the bay and helped herself to the seat next to my bed. “Right,” she said with clear determination and focus. “I know that telling you to ‘be positive’ right now isn’t going to achieve anything apart from pissing you off, so I want you to do something else for me. Right now, you are putting your emotions and feelings first, which are understandably raw and painful, but because you’re letting your emotions rule your behaviour (I’d been intentionally missing physio and OT sessions by this point), you are fundamentally changing the man you are going to be in a year, or in five years.” I’d never seen Kate so focussed, so passionate about what she was trying to convey, the total commitment. “So, what I want you to do is to flip everything on its head. First and foremost, think about the man you want to be in a year’s time, or in five years, think about what he’s doing and where you want him to be. Secondly, act as he would act. Draw inspiration and faith from that future version of yourself and act as he would act. Relegate your emotions and feelings to last place – because I promise that if you do the first two things, you will start to feel better bit by bit.” Kate’s message hit home with its intended impact. I could imagine that future version of myself, free from heartbreak and living with purpose. I wanted to be him. I had to be him. Kate’s words would alter the trajectory of my future.

I’d always had one eye on the future, even at the very beginning of my rehabilitation. I would contemplate how I could still live an independent, physically fit and adventurous lifestyle. Kate’s words had added extra fuel to that fire, compounded by the fact that I was also determined to prove to myself that Ellie had been wrong to leave me. With that in mind, I asked the nursing staff whether it would be possible to have a day’s leave from the hospital to spend some time with Matt and our close friend Harry. I kept details vague, with my true intent flying below the radar. Approval granted, I met Matt and Harry in the car park the next morning, ready for our top-secret excursion together.

A little over an hour later, the three of us arrived at our destination – the Manchester Canoe & Kayak store. Matt and I knew exactly what we were here to do. This was all part of my new five-year plan. Exchanging a quick smile with Matt and Harry, we entered the large industrial unit. It was like opening the cupboard door and walking into Narnia. Within seconds we were surrounded by all different manners of make, model and size of kayak – a whole new world of possibility and opportunity to keep adventure at the core of my life! We'd agreed not to mention to the store's staff that I was still an inpatient on a spinal unit and I made a conscious effort to keep my hospital wristband hidden beneath my sleeve. It didn't take long before Matt and I stumbled upon exactly what we'd come here to find – two matching sea kayaks, the perfect vehicles for the next chapter of our friendship! There was no hard sell required. We purchased both kayaks, along with buoyancy aids, paddles, and all the gear to go with them, and we loaded the boats onto the roof of Matt's Ford Focus before setting off triumphantly back to the hospital. All the gear and absolutely no idea!

Back in physio the next morning, Amy's first question was to ask about yesterday's antics. "So, what was all the secrecy about? Where did you go?" she asked inquisitively.

I hesitated, unsure how best to reveal my latest self-investment to the world. "Amy, could I ask you a question first?" I said cheekily. She smiled and nodded before I continued. "Do you think someone of my injury level could learn to kayak?"

Amy laughed, clearly surprised by the nature of my question. "Oh my God, Darren, what have you done?" she joked nervously. I was committed now. I had to tell her. Reaching for my phone, I found a picture from the day before of Matt and me in front of his car, with the kayaks strapped onto the roof. I passed the phone to Amy and waited for her reaction. "Did you go and buy a bloody kayak?" she exclaimed as she tried to contain her laughter. The look on my face said it all – she knew! I took the broad smile on her face as an overwhelming seal of approval.

Christmas was now only a matter of weeks away and I still had no place to call home before I could be discharged. I was adamant that I could live alone and take care of myself, and with Paula's help I'd been to see several properties – but each came with its challenges to true independent living: too small, too isolated, too inaccessible for a wheelchair. I had to be realistic. For weeks I'd been turning down an offer from my Nan to live with her whilst I got back on my feet (no pun intended), but as other options got ruled out one by one, the only remaining viable choice was to swallow my pride and agree to move in with her. It was another blow to my already fragile self-esteem, but it was also my only chance to avoid spending Christmas and New Year in the hospital.

The 23rd of December would be my final day as a patient at the Midland Centre for Spinal Injuries, a place I had come to call home for close to five months. As I began to pack up the mountains of clutter around my bedspace, I was joined by one of the ward's brilliant Health Care Assistants, Nicky. As we reminisced about the highs and lows of my life since I'd entered the ward fresh from ICU land, she told me that the transition from life at MCSI to the outside world was like "going from the zoo to the jungle". In the zoo, you are cared for, fed and medicated, with a safety blanket wrapped around you. In the jungle, you are living in the wild, solely responsible for your health and vitality. From the relative safety of captivity, the jungle was a scary and intimidating place. But it would be in the jungle that I would rediscover freedom and start to build a new life for myself.

The time had finally come. Having said a series of warm goodbyes to all the staff on the ward, many of whom had become like family, and whom I would miss dearly, there was one last person to say farewell to. Mark was my favourite nurse on the ward, and we'd grown incredibly close. During one of my last evenings as a patient, Mark and I had chatted for hours after he'd finished his shift. At 9 pm his wife had called the ward, concerned as to his whereabouts and fearing the worst. Answering the call, he simply replied, "I'm just sitting here chatting to my friend Darren, aren't I?" Saying goodbye to Mark on that final day was incredibly tough, but also so classically masculine in the way we expressed our emotions. Facing each other, we expertly avoided direct eye contact for fear of seeming overly emotional. Wiping away tears, I said three words I'd not often uttered to other men: "I'll miss you". I meant it wholeheartedly. He'd been there for me from the very start, from admission through to heartbreak. "I'll miss you too, mate," he responded.

This was it. I was about to leave through MCSI's doors for the last time. I paused for a moment as I reached the exit. There was a strong sense of anxiety and trepidation about moving through those doors. Just as I'd struggled to leave my hospital bed for the first time after six weeks of bed rest, the same feelings resurfaced now that I was about to take the next step in my recovery journey. With Mum by my side, it was time to head out into the vast, unknown jungle to live wild and free.

10

RUNNING FREE

I zipped up my buoyancy aid. Adrenaline was pumping through my system. It was the day after my discharge from MCSI and I was about to kayak for the first time in my life. Amidst all the uncertainty surrounding my discharge, my friends had convinced the local leisure centre to allow us to use their main swimming pool to help introduce me to the world of paddling in a safe and controlled environment. With both my and Matt's families in attendance, there was a tangible energy, and an excitement about being part of the next chapter in my journey whilst still in its embryonic stages.

Sitting in my kayak on the edge of the pool, Matt outlined our plan of attack before my maiden voyage commenced. The idea was simple. "We'll slowly slide you in, let you paddle round for five minutes, then Harry and Jack (two of our closest friends) will jump in with you and flip you upside down - just to make sure you can capsize safely," said Matt as he crouched down next to me.

Not even the thought of capsizing could dampen my excitement. "Here we go!" I shouted, joyful as a child, smiling at everyone watching. Mum was smiling too, but I could tell that she was equally, if not more, nervous at seeing her son embark on a new adventure sport so soon after being discharged. Perhaps I couldn't blame her.

Matt, Harry and Jack worked to slide me onto the water incredibly gently and with total control. For the briefest of moments, confident and happy, I glided across the water away from the edge of the pool. The sense of freedom was almost overwhelming as I left my wheelchair behind me, surplus to requirements. No more than two seconds after my maiden voyage began, it ended. As I took my first stroke it caused my body to wobble beneath me, and without any functioning abdominal muscles or the use of my legs to counterbalance the movement of my arms, I found it impossible to avoid a premature dunking. Luckily, my body slipped effortlessly out of the kayak underwater and I swum back to the surface using my arms. Yet, despite capsizing, as I swam back to the surface, I felt more alive than I had since the day of my accident. Emerging from the water, I had a beaming smile plastered across my face. "That was fun! Let's go again?" I shouted as I swam across to the side of the pool, keen to get straight back in.

Christmas Eve 2016 marked the beginning of a new chapter in my journey. Back out into the real world, without the safety net of a team of medical staff behind me, I knew that how my story would evolve was ultimately up to me. It was my responsibility to chase the future version of the person I aspired to be. To be the person who had pulled himself from the wreckage of paralysis and heartbreak to seek new purpose and passion in life, and to emerge stronger from adversity. If nothing else, I remembered that, for four seconds on the 6th of August, I didn't believe I'd see another Christmas with my family. That on its own was worth its weight in gold.

As a newly single man in his mid-20s, moving in with my Nan was a difficult pill to swallow. Don't get me wrong, I love Nan dearly, but with pride at an all-time low, it was yet another blow to my fragile self-esteem to accept that I needed her support. But, in many ways, I quickly realised that it was ultimately the right decision. She was the perfect companion for the transitionary "re-building" stage of my recovery. Now, there would be inevitably a period of adjustment for both of us – Nan had a habit of overcleaning to a large extent, whilst I tended to leave things lying around on the floor (to a large extent). But there was never an issue that couldn't be settled over a cup of tea and a chat. She would burst into my bedroom most mornings with the now familiar wake-up call of, "Fancy a cup of tea love?" Her compassion and energy were boundless. With each day and week that passed, I would learn more about the experiences that defined the person I had simply known as my grandmother. Beyond being just grandchild and grandparent, we started to develop a genuine and loving relationship as friends.

"With every door that closes, a new one opens." I was determined to prove that this adage was as applicable for life with a Spinal Cord Injury as it was for any other situation. There was an expectation from others that I would go through a period of grieving or mourning for what I had lost: a love of mountaineering, a passion for running across the hills and my relationship with Ellie. But, instead, I drew strength from exploring what lay beyond the doors that had opened for me, waiting to be discovered. A new realm of possibility was within my grasp. It would be a challenge to find ways to rediscover the same sense of freedom, fluidity, and independence that I'd been so lucky to have enjoyed before the accident, but I was realistic enough to acknowledge that this would take time (not that patience had ever been a particular attribute of mine!).

It was a crisp winter's morning on the banks of the River Severn in Shrewsbury. Snow crunched underneath my wheels as I made my way across the icy car park toward the ornate boathouse of the Pengwern Boat Club. My friend Sharon happened to be the current captain of the local rowing club and had jumped at the chance of introducing me to her pride and passion. After I arrived, Sharon introduced me to one of the volunteers who helped to run the club's adaptive rowing team. No more than 10 minutes later, Colin had me out of my chair and sitting in an adaptive single-sculling boat. After talking me through the basics and feeling safe in the knowledge that the floating "riggers" on either side of my boat would keep me from capsizing, Colin gently pushed me away from the bank. I glided silently away from my wheelchair, which looked like something of a spare part next to the smiling faces of Colin and Sharon. With each pull, I cut through the misty, still water. Pull. Glide. Pull. Glide. It might have looked awkward, perhaps even clunky to a rowing connoisseur, but it didn't matter to me. As I rowed past the tarmac path I used to run along, I felt the same as I had then. Free.

The first two years after sustaining an SCI is a period within which the body rapidly adjusts, re-adjusts, and potential neurological recovery occurs. Whilst the severity of my injury made further recovery highly improbable, I wanted to leave no stone unturned in my quest to make even the most marginal improvement. There was of course no promise or guarantee that things would change, but in my mind, the worst thing I could do was not try at all. If in two years I was still waiting for a rippling six-pack to suddenly emerge, I'd still be in a better position than I would have been with a negative mindset. If life had taught me anything, it's that we are rewarded for hard work and effort, even in ways we might not appreciate at the time - just like how my experiences with selection and battle camp had forged the mental toughness I now relied upon.

My first move was to pluck up the courage to join a local gym and relegate any social anxiety about people seeing me in a wheelchair for the first time to the back of my mind (Shrewsbury is a very small town). I'd decided before joining that I'd need the support of a personal trainer to help me achieve as much as possible, regardless of my injury. It was during my induction visit that I first met Alex, the Fitness Manager. Heading onto the gym floor, Alex looked at me sitting in my chair, then across at a pull-up bar, and without any hesitation said, "Reckon you could do a pull-up?" Brilliant! I thought. At that moment I knew that Alex would be someone who would help me to truly test the limits of what was possible, and most importantly, I could sense that he wouldn't try and wrap me in cotton wool and play it safe with our selection of exercises.

So, back to that first pull-up. As luck would have it, we found a way of making it possible if Alex stood in front of me and braced my knees. However, as I heaved my body out of my chair and up to the bar above, my arms shaking with the effort, it appeared that my trousers hadn't gotten the memo and fell in the opposite direction. Unfortunately, I didn't have any underwear on (in hospital I'd grown used to not wearing any). Thankfully, the three ladies on the rowing machines opposite didn't take offence to my impromptu rendition of the Full Monty. With my trousers safely back around my hips, Alex and I moved around the gym trying different exercises, both of us learning about how my injury affected different types of movement. Nothing was put into the "too hard" pile, simply into the "we'll have to work on that a bit more" pile, as Alex would put it. At the end of our first session together, he looked at me and said, "Right, let's get you to the Paralympics!" The sky was the limit!

The 6th of August 2016 also impacted the trajectory of my career. Having worked for Shropshire Council since moving back from London in 2013, I was no more than three weeks away from leaving and starting my training to become a history teacher at a local secondary school when I fell from the top of World's End. Fate had other plans. Thankfully, and to the credit of Shropshire Council and my boss Sam Williams, I would have a job to return to whenever I felt ready. I knew that going back to work would provide me with some semblance of normality and a connection back to my old life, but I also knew that it would come with challenges – both physically and emotionally. More than anything else, I didn't want to be treated differently. I was still me, still the same overly optimistic, adventurous soul who struggled with office life; I hadn't changed a bit in that regard. Having pleaded my case with the Council that I was ready to return to work just three weeks after leaving the hospital, I found myself back in the office once more, surrounded by those who had kept me company during many an hour in the weeks following my accident. For those individuals, I will be forever grateful.

• • •

Eventually, as winter gave way to spring and temperatures dared to climb into double digits, it was time to make the leap of faith from kayaking in the relatively safe confines of a swimming pool to exploring the local rivers and lakes. With Matt and Harry by my side, the pillars of strength they had been since the day my world turned upside down, what could go wrong? We planned to explore a stretch of the River Severn close to the village of Melverley in North Shropshire. On the day of our adventure, and true to form, it was an unexpected obstacle before we'd even started that proved to be the most problematic – a locked farmer's gate leading down to the water's edge. Two minutes later, as Matt was holding me in his arms and passing me across the gate to Harry waiting on the other side, like oversized baggage at an airport, a family of four walked past with their dog. "Gorgeous morning, isn't it?" I shouted across to them as I awkwardly waved hello. With my wheelchair out of sight behind the bush next to Harry, God knows what they thought was going on down at the river in Melverley that day.

Once I'd managed to stubbornly wheel myself across the muddy field and down to the water's edge, I felt a combination of excitement and trepidation building within me. Watching the flow of the river as it ran from my right to left, I knew that this was a significant step up from the confined, safe pastures of the local swimming pool. Capsizing here would be a different type of problem altogether. Transferring down into my kayak, I set my backrest up behind me, made sure that my legs were free from any entrapment beneath the cockpit, and tried to shake off my nerves as I waited for our adventure to begin. My heart was well and truly pounding! Matt stood waist-high in the river next to me, helping to steady my kayak before letting me drift away from the bank. "How's that feeling balance-wise, mate?" he asked.

"Yep," I replied, as I took my first stroke.

"No, I said how's that feeling balance-wise?" he asked once more.

"Yep," came my response.

Frustrated that he couldn't get a logical answer from me, Matt insisted, "Yep *what*? Does that mean you're good or you're not?". The truth was, I was so focussed on keeping my balance that I'd suffered some form of temporary conversational paralysis. My entire body and mind at that moment had one single reason for existing – staying upright!

I entered the pull of the river's current, like gravity being drawn by an invisible force deeper into uncharted territory. I ignored the urge to try and fight against it, instead letting the river gently guide me downstream. In that moment, I felt so incredibly connected to nature, her life force exerting control over my body in this small, floating piece of fibreglass we call a kayak. This was adventure. This was what I loved. Matt and Harry had jumped into their kayaks and were shadowing me like guardian angels, ready to swoop in at any sign of disaster or struggle. My paddle cut peacefully through the dark water. With each stroke, I felt a growing sense of freedom and liberation. Now 200 metres downstream, as the flow of the river guided us around the first bend, the nervous tension in my face had lifted and was replaced by a relaxed, contented smile. Harry was meanwhile relishing his designated role of "safety boat" with full enthusiasm and vigour. As Matt and I chatted side by side, we suddenly heard an almighty roar of "SAFETY BOAT COMING THROUGH!" as Harry paddled furiously past us in a show of speed and power that resulted in the first little waves I'd ever had to deal with. There certainly would have been a sense of laughable irony had I capsized thanks to the antics of the safety boat!

Life had, undeniably, changed since the day of my accident. Yet, as I paddled side by side with my best friends on the river that day, my wheelchair forgotten and out of sight beyond a bend, I realised that in so many ways it hadn't changed at all. We were still three best friends, brought closer together by shared experience, still carrying that flame for adventure, and an unbreakable bond of friendship. Life and friendship would flourish in the face of adversity – of this I was certain.

11

DREAMING OF TOKYO

"Think about where you want to be in a year, or in five years' time, Darren – and aim for that!" Those had been Kate's words as she helped me to come to terms with and move on from the breaking apart of my relationship with Ellie. Even amidst the uncertainty and heartbreak of that time, I still dared to dream. I'd watched coverage of the Rio Paralympics as I neared the final weeks of my time on bed rest, and it had been the perfect antidote to any notion that my life would be somehow limited by my disability. Only a matter of weeks after the Games had finished, I received a letter from Paralympian, Nick Beighton. In his letter, Nick explained that he was a member of Great Britain's Paracanoe squad (sprint kayaking), and he included a leaflet titled "The Road to Tokyo", which was aimed at finding the next generation of athletes to compete at the Tokyo 2020 Paralympic Games. A seed had been planted.

Six months had passed since I first received Nick's letter. Above the TV in my bedroom at Nan's house hung a framed picture of Mount Everest. Tucked into the corner of the frame was the very same Road to Tokyo leaflet Nick had sent all those months ago. It was my way of acknowledging that I would need to pursue a new "Mount Everest" in my life, whilst also paying homage to my past. Now that I was six months further into this new journey and had already overcome some of the initial physical and emotional challenges, I felt ready to do more than just sit and look at the leaflet from across my room. I booked myself to attend the squad's next selection day, or Talent Identification Day as it was known, which was a matter of weeks away, at the end of June. It was time to dream of Tokyo!

Sitting at the front of a cramped conference room alongside the other would-be athletes who had put themselves forward for selection, it reminded me of turning up at the start of the selection process to join the SAS Reserve. We were welcomed to the High-Performance Training Centre for Great Britain's Paralympic sprint kayak programme by Steve Train, Head Coach. I had no idea what to expect from the day, or what it would entail, but as we watched a montage of the team's recent performances at the Rio Paralympic Games, I was ready to give everything I had to prove that I belonged here – as I once had across the windswept hills of the Brecon Beacons, pushing myself beyond my physical limits.

The talent identification process aimed to systematically test our suitability for the High-Performance programme and determine whether we had the raw materials from which they could forge a future Paralympic champion. My day could have started better. At the beginning of my assessment with the team's physiotherapist, he revealed that they had assessed several other candidates with my level of spinal injury, but that none of them had managed to meet the required standards. Somehow, I felt emboldened by his comments, as if a gauntlet had been thrown down – a "hold my beer" moment, if you will. Over the course of the next 30 minutes, I was asked to replicate a series of exercises that would give him an indication of my balance, core function and physiological capacity.

"Okay Darren, go ahead and sit back in your chair now," came his instruction as he finished the testing. I was impatient to hear his assessment. "Impressive. Impressive for someone who has a T6 spinal injury," came his feedback, accompanied by a slightly perplexed expression on his face. Success!

There was an eclectic mix of injuries and disabilities taking part in this first stage of the selection process: wheelchair users, amputees on prosthetic limbs, individuals with neurological conditions. Each of us was there to prove that we had what it would take to become an elite athlete. The group spent the rest of the morning on a series of gym-based assessments that would test the physical attributes required of a sprint kayaker: explosive power and cardiovascular fitness. I instantly clicked with Jen, an anaesthetist who had been in the RAF and had recently competed at the Invictus Games. As we performed each exercise, the team's strength and conditioning coach recorded our scores. I'd worked my way through the initial tests: press-ups, tricep dips, bench press, but now it was time for the big one… pull-ups. If my trousers could manage to stay around my hips, I was confident that I could beat my target of six reps. Hanging below the bar, I waited for my cue to begin.

"3, 2, 1, GO!"

I pulled my chest up to the bar for the first rep. I felt strong. My work with Alex was starting to pay dividends. By the time my arms were overwhelmed by lactic acid, I had completed nine pull-ups – I was elated!

After a brief break for lunch, we continued on to a series of further assessments, before finishing the day with one final trial, which would be the most indicative of my future chances of success or failure. Leaving the gym, we walked down to the team's boat shed. The walls of the building were adorned with sprawling Union Jack flags; if I needed further inspiration, this was it. Our final test was a "best effort" 200-metre sprint on a kayak ergo machine. It was soon my turn. I took up position on the ergo, my legs bent slightly out in front of me, and a strap around my core secured me to the seat. This was it. One last chance to show my potential.

"3, 2, 1, GO!" came the call from Steve Train. I drove my right-hand blade forward, then my left, then my right, accelerating with each drive forward. The cables offered greater resistance than I'd expected, and by the 100-metre mark, I could feel lactic acid burning in my arms and shoulders. I dug deep. Keep pushing, Darren. With shouts of encouragement from the group, I dragged myself across the 200-metre mark. I was spent – I had nothing left and could do nothing more. My future was now in the hands of Steve and his team. It would be two weeks until I would hear back from them with their decision.

Waiting impatiently to learn my fate, I was invited to speak at an event in London to share my story publicly for the first time. The thought of speaking about my darkest and most trying moments with a room full of strangers was an intimidating prospect, but I also recognised that telling my story could benefit others and show that adversity does not define our outcome – our actions do. Arriving at the venue in the heart of Soho, joined by one of my closest friends Jack, we encountered the evening's first challenge… a broken lift. Once again embracing an "adapt and overcome" mindset, and fortunate enough to have physically strong friends, I was carried up a winding staircase (still sitting in my chair) by Jack and another friend of ours. I entered the room looking like an Egyptian Pharaoh. It was one hell of a way to announce my arrival.

My slot that evening was part of a series of talks organised by adventurer, Dave Cornthwaite. The series was titled "Yes Stories" and was designed to bring together human-interest stories of individuals who had taken the path less travelled, or who had triumphed over adversity. I hadn't rehearsed my talk. My tactic was simple – talk openly, honestly, and from the heart. I had the images from my accident and recovery to help illustrate the narrative as I wanted, and I just hoped that the audience would connect with my story.

I began my talk with a caveat, letting everyone know that "this is the first time I've openly spoken about my journey, so I do apologise if the emotions, for me, are at times a little raw." I was heartened to see lots of empathetic, smiling faces looking back at me. There were moments where I'd reach a certain point in my story, like the second I began to fall from the rockface, or when Ellie walked out through the hospital doors for the last time, and I'd have to stop. I'd tilt my head back as if I was somehow hoping to stop the tears from coming by draining them backwards. Yet, as I looked out at the crowd with a sense of embarrassment that emotions were getting the better of me, I saw a room full of people with tears in their eyes, as if they were living this journey with me. It was then that I realised it was okay to be emotional, raw, and vulnerable. No one was judging me, only supporting me.

When I came to the most recent aspects of my story, whether that was jumping into a kayak the day after my discharge from MCSI, getting passed over a gate post like oversized baggage by my closest friends, or putting myself forward for selection to the GB Paracanoe team, I loved how the room laughed and celebrated those small but important milestones in my recovery. Within seconds of my talk ending, the sound of moving chairs reverberated over the wooden floor as everyone got to their feet in applause. I was utterly overwhelmed, exhilarated, and exhausted. It had been an incredibly intimate and emotive experience for me, and to have shared some of my darkest moments with a room full of strangers had been a big step forward in my emotional healing process. It was like free therapy – with a round of applause at the end!

12

NEW HORIZONS

Two weeks had passed since I'd attended the talent identification day for the Paracanoe team, and whilst I waited eagerly to hear from British Canoeing, I found myself struggling emotionally with some aspects of returning to my old life. I'd always been the type of person who found it hard to sit down for any length of time, often opting for a lunchtime workout to get some endorphins firing between meetings. Now that I was a "full-time sitter", I felt like I had lost a part of my identity, and my sense of independence diminished.

Sitting in the office late one afternoon, I was overcome by a wave of sadness. I took myself out of the room before anyone could see the emotion in my eyes and went up to an unoccupied meeting room above. Staring at my reflection in the tinted glass window, it felt like my wings had been clipped, my horizons curtailed. Careful not to let myself get swept away by this wave of negativity, I reached for my phone to help change my mindset. "Missed Call – New Voicemail" flashed across the screen. I pressed play. "Hi Darren, it's Steve from British Canoeing. I wanted to call to let you know that we would like to invite you to the next stage of selection…" I looked back at my reflection in the window, feeling a renewed confidence and determination.

The next stage of selection was to be staggered over the course of six months and would involve a rigorous training and assessment programme. Pertinently, candidates could be released at any stage. Nothing less than total commitment was expected. Arriving on a particularly wet and windy day at the National Water Sports Centre, I was met by Steve Train and joined two of the other successful candidates down at the lake's edge. I was pleasantly surprised to see Jen again, as well as a Welsh medical student called Will I'd also chatted to, who was a below-knee amputee. After a brief catch-up, Steve outlined the plan of attack for the coming days, weeks and months. His message was clear: this was our opportunity to showcase why we'd be suitable for this programme.

Keen to impress, I made as little fuss as possible transferring down from my wheelchair onto the rubber matting of the pontoon and across to the waiting kayak. The pontoon itself resembled something of an apocalyptic disaster zone with prosthetic feet, legs and wheelchairs strewn across the platform. That was the charm of the Paracanoe squad, everyone had a story to tell, but none had been defined by the adversity they had faced – they had triumphed over it. Steve crouched down next to me, his hand steadying my kayak as I fought to gain my balance. Every inch of functioning muscle strained to stabilise my body as I wobbled from side to side atop the unstable kayak. I felt like I was sitting on a plate of jelly. Steve looked at me with a reassuring smile, "Got it?" he inquired.

"Getting there," I responded with a measure of fake confidence. With Jen and Will gliding elegantly away from the pontoon ahead of me, and finally balanced in my kayak, I dared to take the first strokes of my Paracanoe journey.

As I drifted away from the pontoon, I kept my hands low and in the most stable position. Each stroke barely scraped the surface of the water. My internal monologue was simply a repetition of the words "Don't fall in, Darren" but it felt like I was sitting on top of a bucking bronco that was determined to throw me off at the first opportunity. I'd made it no more than ten metres before my weight rolled too far to the left, and my delicate grip on balance was undone. SPLOSH! This was a familiar feeling. Determined not to let a setback deter my chances of success, I swam across to the riverbank with the kayak hooked under my arm, ready to try again. As Steve hauled me out of the water, he asked whether I wanted to get showered and into some dry clothes. "No, I'm absolutely fine, let's go again," I replied. And so began a cycle that we would repeat four times that morning. But, with each attempt, I made it further and further from the pontoon. 20 metres. 30 metres. 40 metres. Emerging with a smile on my face after the fourth unscheduled dunking of the morning, I knew that, if nothing else, Steve couldn't doubt my commitment.

By the end of my second day, I had quite possibly set a record for the greatest number of capsizes in 48 hours. With each minute on the water, I was learning more about how my injury impacted my ability to balance, and how I could use what I was still able to control to stay the right way up. Psychologically, the hardest element was watching Jen and Will paddle off into the distance far ahead of me – it was hard not to feel frustrated. As I sat down with Steve the next day for my first progress review, he opened cryptically with "Darren, we were surprised." I waited with bated breath for him to elaborate. "Most people of your injury level don't make it off the pontoon on day one… at all!" he said with a friendly laugh. The thought had never occurred to me that I might be exceeding expectations. "Keep up the good work," were his closing words as we left the conference room. For the first time in a long time, I felt proud of who I was.

Over the course of the next three months, I would find myself back at the National Water Sports Centre almost every other week for further training and assessment before I could properly move onto the Development Pathway. The positive dynamic and camaraderie between me, Jen and Will only deepened as we got to know more about each other, and the events that had led us each to this point. Will was only 17 when he had to make the life-changing decision to have the lower half of his left leg amputated due to bone cancer, Jen was a doctor in the Royal Air Force until a skiing accident left her with a complex spinal cord injury. As part of our assessments, we had to be put through a medical classification process to determine within which of the three Paracanoe categories we would sit within: KL1 being the most impaired function (mainly spinal injury patients), KL3 as the least impaired (mainly lower leg amputees/impairments). To no great surprise, I was classified as KL1, whilst Jen was KL2 and Will KL3.

Being classified as KL1 helped me to mentally rationalise the fact that my development rate would be slower than Jen and Will's, and that I had to stop trying to draw direct comparisons to them. So, whilst Jen and Will floated off down the lake to work on more advanced skills with another coach, Steve and I would stick to the sheltered western edge in an area we affectionately termed the "kids' pool". Despite best intentions, my relationship with capsizing continued in earnest. Steve would diligently do his best to impart knowledge and direction from the pontoon's edge as I gingerly paddled back and forth to the far bank of the lake. With each failure came a learning point, and with each failure came a choice: do you give up or do you persevere? As the weeks progressed, and as I doggedly persevered, my technique gradually improved. I started to make tangible progress.

It was fast approaching the first anniversary of the day life had irreversibly changed. I couldn't believe that the events I could still vividly remember from the accident had happened 12 months ago, the panicked images of those darkest moments. So many aspects of my life changed or had to be adapted in the intervening period. Yet, as I reflected on my journey thus far, there were so many positives to celebrate and so many reasons to be hopeful, even optimistic, for the future. Yes, there had been moments where emotions had felt overwhelming – be they anger, frustration or heartbreak – but what mattered most was that I'd stayed true to the promise I made as I lay broken at the bottom of the rockface at World's End on the 6th of August 2016 – I'd never given up.

With my family by my side, we marked the first anniversary at the top one of the many stunning hills in South Shropshire, watching the sun melt into the horizon. There was no sadness for what had been lost, simply a sense of pride for what we had overcome as a family, a family that I thought I would lose in the seconds after that fateful ledge crumbled beneath my feet. Dad summed it up perfectly that night: "Well, it's been one hell of a year son!"

It certainly had.

13

THE MIRACLE

"How did it feel to be told that you wouldn't walk again?" came the question from a student in Year 10. I hesitated, slightly unsure how to best articulate a response to the packed assembly hall. The truth was that I'd been told twice: once in intensive care the day after my surgery, and then again six weeks later as I came to the end of bed rest. Even as I was shown the scans from the day of my accident, with the severity of damage plain to see, I hadn't truly believed that I'd taken my last steps. If anyone could defy the odds, surely it would be me. But, as the months passed and my condition didn't change, I remembered the words of my spinal surgeon: "You need to accept it and move on with your new life, Darren."

I looked across the room to the student who had asked the question and answered them openly and honestly. "When they first told me I didn't believe them. I never quite gave up hope that a miracle could happen, but logic told me I needed to move forward and not look back." In the two and a half years since I was told that I'd never walk again, I had indeed moved forward with my life. As the dream of walking faded, new ambitions and hopes had risen in its place. I had surfed off the coast of California, learnt to sit-ski and was chasing my greatest dream – qualifying for and competing at the Paralympic Games in Tokyo 2020.

For more than a year, my life had been split between Nottingham and Shrewsbury. To chase the dream of representing Great Britain, I was training three days a week at the National Water Sports Centre and the rest of the week at home in Shrewsbury (Nan's garage had been overtaken by a kayak ergo machine). Being part of the Paracanoe development team had allowed me to be surrounded by some of the most elite athletes in the world, many of whom were incredibly supportive of my development: Emma Wiggs, Rob Oliver, and of course Nick Beighton, whose letter to me in the hospital had been the very reason for starting this journey. My aim for the year ahead was clear: to race internationally for the first time.

It had been another wet and blustery day's training at Nottingham, and I sat on the physio studio's rubber floor doing some light stretching before making the two-hour drive home. Finishing my last stretch, I aimlessly scrolled through Instagram for a minute or two until my phone started to ring. The number that flashed up on my screen started with the area code 01539, and had Cumbria written below. My first inclination was to ignore the call; I was already pressed for time if I was going to beat the traffic home. But something told me to answer it. On the other end of the line was a well-spoken, elderly-sounding gentleman. He introduced himself as Paul Adorian, a businessman from the Lake District.

"Darren, the reason I'm calling today is to say that I have just finished reading your online blog about your incredible journey, and I wondered if I could ask you a very particular question?" Curious as to what his question might be, I thanked him for taking the time to read about my story and said I'd of course be happy to answer any questions.

"Have you ever thought or dreamt about walking again?"

"Of course," I replied slightly perplexed as to the strangeness of the question coming from a stranger. I continued by explaining that life had, however, taken on new hopes and aspirations as the dream of walking had faded.

"That was what I was hoping you might say, Darren," Paul said, pausing, and clearly taking his time before speaking again. "My wife Ruth and I have seen these incredible robotic machines, I think they're called 'exoskeletons', that are helping people like you to walk again. Have you seen them in action?" came his follow-up.

I knew exactly what Paul was referring to as I had seen the "ReWalk Exoskeleton" up close at a conference earlier that year. I had watched in awe as a man paralysed from the chest down, just as I was, walked past me and off into the distance. The moment presented a cruel paradox: whilst I had just witnessed that walking again was now within the realms of possibility, the cost of each ReWalk device exceeded £80,000. I'd never be able to afford one of my own.

"Darren, what would you say if Ruth and I offered to buy one of these machines for you?" came Paul's voice over the phone, jolting me from my thoughts. I froze – both verbally and literally. Surely, I'd got something wrong here, it was all sounding far too good to be true. For a moment I even contemplated which of my friends could a) sound like an elderly man from Cumbria and b) think that this was a hilarious practical joke. My hesitation did not go unnoticed by Paul.

"Well, how about it? If we were to use some of our money to buy you your very own Re-Walk Exoskeleton. What would you say?" he repeated for my benefit a second time.

Bloody hell, I had heard him right! I tripped and stuttered over my words as I struggled to articulate what should have been the simplest answer I'd ever given in my life: Yes!

"Paul, I don't know what to say," came my response, still suspended in a state of disbelief and shock.

"How about 'Yes'?" came his voice over the phone.

I responded hesitantly, my voice filled with doubt. "Yes?"

"Fantastic! Leave it with me and I'll be in touch soon. Take care for now." The phone line went dead. Paul had hung up. I sat there in disbelief, vaguely noticing the expressions of intrigue on the faces of those around me. I looked up and said, "I think someone has just offered to buy me some £80,000 robotic legs!" Judging by the stares of confusion and disbelief, you would have thought I'd just told them I was about to walk on the moon.

I drove home that afternoon still trying to convince myself that Paul's phone call had happened. Arriving back at Nan's, there was nothing I wanted more than to share my news along the lines of "You will NEVER guess what has just happened!" but I was incredibly conscious not to raise anyone else's hopes at the risk of this all turning out badly. As she flicked on the kettle, Nan asked, "How was your day love?"

I considered my response for a second, before replying, "I think something pretty incredible happened today, but I can't say anything just yet."

She looked across the kitchen at me as I stood up in the frame I'd brought home from the hospital and responded, "Ooh, sounds exciting."

It had been two and a half years since Nan had seen me walk. I just hoped that, now, it wouldn't have been the last time.

Two days passed since the call, and I found myself increasingly doubtful, even sceptical, that what had seemed too good to be true might indeed turn out to be a promise left unfulfilled. Then, as I sat on my bed watching an episode of

Game of Thrones on my laptop, my phone rang. It was another unfamiliar number. I answered the call.

"Isn't it fantastic? I bet you couldn't believe it when Paul called you…" came a voice. I didn't recognise who it was at first until it dawned on me that the voice belonged to Steve Russell, a sales rep from ReWalk Robotics, whom I'd met the day I saw the man with an injury like mine walk across a stunned conference room.

I had one burning question… "How did all this come about? How does Paul even know who the hell I am?"

Over the course of the next few minutes, Steve filled me in on all the missing elements to the story: how he had been approached out of the blue by Paul, who wanted to find a way in which he and his wife Ruth could help transform someone's life; how they had been inspired by the footage they'd seen of the ReWalk on TV and how Steve had sent them a copy of "Strength through Adversity", which I'd kept since my injury. All these little pieces in the puzzle had slotted together and led to Paul calling me two days ago.

Once Steve and I finished speaking, and with a plan of action in place for how and when I might take my first steps again, I could shout from the rooftops with full conviction that this was happening. I called excitedly downstairs to my grandmother. "Nan, you will NEVER guess what has just happened!" (I had to shout twice as Nan's hearing is less than reliable.) Her words that afternoon were to be mirrored by so many over the course of the coming weeks: "There are good people in this world after all," she said, wiping away tears as she hugged me. The dream that I had stubbornly held onto for so long, against all odds and despite what all the doctors had told me, was about to come true. Not in the way I had once envisaged, but in a way that was a testament to the uniquely human trait of empathy.

A little over a month had passed since I'd received that life-changing phone call from a total stranger. Mum and I were making the short drive to Stourbridge from Shrewsbury. It promised to be a momentous day. We were en route to the NPP Neuro Group, where I would walk for the very first time in my ReWalk Exoskeleton. My emotions were a concoction of disbelief, excitement, nervousness, and perhaps even an element of fear. As we arrived at NPP's studio, we were met by my physio, Peter, and shown through to the front studio where Steve from ReWalk's stood, beaming at us. He pointed across the studio to where my exoskeleton was sitting in an upright position. The slim, black outline of the robotic machine gave it a futuristic edge. I was five metres away from walking again.

"I bet you can't believe this is happening?" Steve joked as he readied the exoskeleton for me to transfer into from my wheelchair. Once I'd transferred across, Steve began to clip in and tighten the series of straps that would secure me to the device at my knees, thighs, and waist. He talked me through the series of mechanical processes that would see the device stand me up and enable me to begin walking across the room. I realised I was staring in disbelief, completely overwhelmed. I nodded at Steve as he finished his instructions before strapping the device's smartwatch to my wrist. Finally, he passed me the two crutches I would need to stand up and maintain balance whilst walking.

"Okay, so once I press the 'stand' button on the smartwatch, the device will beep three times and then stand you up on the fourth beep. As it does, you need to push up with your crutches to help the device bring you vertical. I'll be in front of you to make sure that you don't fall forward. Ready?" Steve said as he moved to stand in front of me.

"Yep," I muttered in excited, nervous anticipation for what

was about to happen.

Steve selected the button on my smartwatch. The exoskeleton made three distinct beeps. I readied myself for the fourth beep. When it sounded, I fixed my sight at a point on the top of the wall ahead of me and pushed down on the crutches as the device moved beneath me. Within seconds I was standing bolt upright. My heart was beating furiously. I took a few seconds to get accustomed to this strange new way of standing, steadying my balance, and shifting the crutches slightly out in front of me as I stood back at 6ft tall. I looked up from my feet (which seemed a long way down) to see Mum smiling with emotion across the room. "Remember to breathe, Darren," came her loving, motherly reminder.

Steve kept proceedings moving along by providing his calm, concise, and reassuring instruction as to how we'd work together to make the exoskeleton walk. I needed to start by leaning slightly forward, before beginning to subtly shift my weight from one foot to the other as the device would replicate the motion of moving one foot forward, and then the other. I took a deep breath. "Here goes nothing!" I joked, with a slight warble of nerves in my voice. The next few minutes of my life were momentous, seconds I will never forget.

I allowed my body to lean forward onto my crutches, and the exoskeleton made a distinctly robotic "zhoop" noise as the device began to lift my right leg, bending at the knee, before swinging my foot forward and planting it securely on the floor. I couldn't believe what I'd just seen. Then, as I shifted my weight to the right, my left leg began to lift, before also planting my foot on the ground in front of me. There was an element of fear, of feeling vulnerable and precarious standing up on my feet and moving forward again after so long. Yet, at the same time, it was exhilarating and overwhelming emotionally. Tears began to form in my eyes. I was taking the most significant steps of my life, quite literally; steps I'd come to think I'd never take again. The device's robotic noise echoed in the empty studio as I continued to stride forward, gaining confidence. Before I knew it, I was getting closer to the white wall at the end of the studio, but I'd forgotten what Steve had said as to how I could stop walking!

"4, 3, 2, 1…" Steve counted me down, expecting me to bring the device to a stop. "Lean forward, lean forward, LEAN FORWARD!" he cried with ever-increasing urgency as I headed step by step closer to a collision on my maiden voyage.

I desperately tried to lean forward, but I was now a matter of inches from the wall. My right leg lifted, and as it swung forward, THUD!, I kicked the wall. Thankfully, the exoskeleton took this as its cue to stop walking. There was a collective sigh of relief across the room. Steve and I couldn't help but burst out into fits of laughter. Peter joked from across the room, "I hope you'll be paying to repair that wall, Darren." Sorry, Peter!

After a little shuffling and spinning on the spot with Steve holding the front of me and the device, I stood facing back across the room to where my wheelchair sat, unoccupied. It was an incredibly surreal, touching moment.

"Come on Julie, come and give your son a big hug," Steve said, beckoning to Mum.

She approached cautiously, clearly anxious about coming in too strong and accidentally knocking me off balance. She wrapped her arms around me, holding me tightly. After a few seconds, I could tell that she had me; I wasn't falling anywhere. I relaxed my hold on the crutches, letting them fall to my side as I stood and held Mum tightly for the first time in over two and a half years. I let my head drop down to rest on top of hers. It felt like the last few years had never happened, I was simply hugging my Mum as I always had. As we joked and laughed and stood next to each other, Steve took what would become one of my favourite pictures of Mum and me.

Over the course of the next hour, I stomped back and forth across the small studio, building confidence and pride with each step. I'd once made a promise to myself to never give up, no matter what the future had in store, but I'd very nearly given up on ever walking again. It was a poignant and moving moment on my recovery journey. Sitting back down at the end of the session, I was utterly exhausted but already couldn't wait to walk again. We said our goodbyes to Peter and Steve, and as I turned to exit the studio, Steve called over from the opposite side of the room: "Wait, are you not taking these with you?" He gestured towards the exoskeleton. We all laughed. It still felt so surreal that they were mine, and even more surreal given the circumstances under which this all came about, thanks to the generosity of two strangers.

Later that evening I gave Paul a call to thank him and Ruth for what they had done for me. It was because of them, and the family and friends for whom seeing me walk again was such a miracle, that the steps I took that afternoon would be the first of thousands to come. I struggled to find the words to adequately articulate to Paul how much that day had meant to me, how much his and Ruth's generosity had meant to me and my family. In response, he simply said, "We're just glad that we could help, Darren." I insisted that I wanted to go up to the Lake District to meet them and thank them in person. Paul politely pushed back. "In time Darren. Please, there's no rush, we're just glad that we could do this for you. Just enjoy walking again." There was nothing I could say to convince him otherwise. They did this for me, not for their self-gratification.

Over a year later that Paul eventually relented to my requests to go and visit him and Ruth in the Lake District. Arriving at their house in the foothills above Lake Windermere, I met the man who changed my life for the first time. He introduced me to Ruth, who was living with the latter stages of Motor Neuron Disease. Regardless, there was such unconditional, unbreakable love between the two of them, no matter the challenges they faced, and in how they were able to communicate given Ruth's condition. Having faced the hard truth that no amount of money could improve her MND prognosis, the couple committed to using their money to change the lives of others. It was an honour and privilege to have met and to know them.

It was only a matter of months later that I got the sad news of Ruth's passing. My heart broke for Paul. He was totally, unconditionally in love with the incredible woman he'd met many years before, long before MND had become part of their journey. I was honoured when Paul asked me to be part of Ruth's commemoration service. It was my opportunity to stand in front of a packed church and to say, wholeheartedly, that without the incredible woman that we were mourning that day, I wouldn't be standing there. There is also a woman called Lucy who, after being paralysed 10 years ago, has walked again for the first time thanks to Ruth.

"We are part of Ruth's eternal legacy," I said with a tear in my eye.

14

THE MISSING PIECE

Life was moving in an exciting and promising direction. I'd discovered a powerful sense of drive and purpose as I chased my aspirational dream of competing at the Paralympic Games. Against all the odds, I'd even learnt to walk again. The pieces of the puzzle were starting to come together. But there remained one missing piece that I feared I'd never be able to find again – love.

I'd long since recovered from the physical trauma of my accident. The trailing scars along my arm and down my back were now simply worn as badges of pride for what I'd come through. In contrast, my emotional wounds were more complex and layered with more than a singular trauma. I had been fortunate enough to have processed the emotional distress from my accident, as well as coming to terms with my disability, relatively swiftly. Yet, there was still a gaping, raw psychological wound that hadn't healed since having my heart broken. The relationship with Ellie falling apart had left me with a deep-rooted sense of inadequacy and a fear of trusting someone not to break my heart. In short, I was afraid of being left again.

I wanted to be happy. I wanted to find someone who could love me for who I was and to whom my disability didn't matter.

But I had developed an unhealthy habit of self-sabotaging any chance of a new relationship (both consciously and subconsciously). Whilst I downloaded the online dating apps Tinder and Bumble, hoping that they'd be some form of quick-fix emotional plaster, it only proved to me that I wasn't ready to entrust someone with my happiness. It seemed easier and less painful to be alone – to push people away. That was all about to change.

Let me ask you a question. Do you remember your teenage crush? I mean the person you adored more than anything, but the planets never seemed to align and before you realised, it was too late. For me, that was a girl called Tesni-Jayne Taylor. I was 18, had just returned to Shrewsbury from a gap year in Australia, and I was looking to earn some money before heading off to university in the autumn. As fate would have it, I got a job as a waiter at the local Pizza Hut. Arriving for one of my very first shifts, I was introduced to a beautiful waitress known as "TJ". Her smile was infectious, and her short brunette hair accentuated her warm, attractive features. Over the course of the next few months, my heart would always beat a little bit faster if I saw her name next to mine on the shift rota. But I never had the confidence or self-belief to consider for a moment that she might be interested in me – "She'd go for someone cooler than me," was the go-to excuse I'd make for not making a move. Before I knew it, it was too late.

10 years had passed since I'd graced the tables of Pizza Hut with my woefully inconsistent waitering service, and life had taken me on its rollercoaster voyage of expected and unexpected journeys (as you well know by now). In all the years that had passed, I'd never forgotten about TJ, but as far as I was concerned, even after a decade, she still wouldn't be interested in me. Arriving in Oxford one evening ahead of a talk to a

business the next day, I checked into my hotel before heading out for something to eat. As I sat at a table for one waiting for my food to arrive, I opened Tinder on my phone hoping that some mindless swiping would serve as a temporary antidote to my feelings of abject loneliness. To my stunned surprise, the first profile that I saw was beautifully familiar – it was TJ! With my heart skipping a beat, I swiped right to say "Yes!" to this potential match. Now was the hard part – waiting to find out if she would swipe yes for me…

My talk the next morning had gone well, and as I prepared to drive back to Shrewsbury, I saw that I had a notification from Tinder – a new message. Better yet, it was from TJ! "Fancy seeing you here!" read her message. Somehow, I managed to "play it cool" as I refrained from replying that very second (which I wanted to). I then spent the entirety of the two-hour drive home trying to craft the perfect response. A response that would project an air of confidence and self-belief (which I didn't have), and a response that wouldn't seem overly keen (which I was). I failed at both.

With my heart on my sleeve, I replied, "It certainly is! I never thought I'd see you on Tinder – I always imagined you'd be in a happy, long-term relationship! How are you?" Oh, Darren… Only time would tell if I'd blown it with the very first message moments after a chance reconnection after more than a decade apart.

As chance would have it, I hadn't blown it. Over the course of the next few weeks, we would move from talking on Tinder to talking every day on WhatsApp, and then making plans for what would be our first date. Our only potential stumbling block was that TJ now lived and worked as a teacher in Hampshire, three or so hours from Shrewsbury. With the aid of Google Maps, we happened upon Warwick Castle as the picturesque backdrop for a halfway date the next weekend. It wasn't long before I found myself waiting nervously next to the castle's main entrance for TJ to arrive. Glancing to my right, I saw her walking across from me with a smile on her face. She looked as beautiful as I remembered. The short brunette hairstyle I had once known had been replaced by long flowing blonde hair, but there was no changing her seemingly eternal bright blue eyes. I couldn't believe that I'd waited so long to see her again.

Despite my nerves, it didn't take long for the conversation to start flowing as we walked beside towering stone walls on our way to the castle's main building. If there was ever an awkward silence, I knew that we could reminisce about our time serving overpriced oven pizzas, but we didn't have to. We spoke with the familiarity and fondness of two people who hadn't just spent the last ten years as distant strangers. The beautiful surroundings in which we found ourselves, which radiated the romance of a bygone era, only added to the promising mood our date had started with.

As we approached the ornate archway into the castle, there was a flight of stairs separating us from the main lobby. An attendant made her way down to us and started directing us to the disabled lift. I tried my best to hide my embarrassment at the situation, but my insecurities flared. Perhaps this would be the moment that TJ would realise dating me would come with potential hurdles and roadblocks. But, without a moment's hesitation, she looked down at me with a glint of excitement in her eye and said, "Look at us, getting the VIP treatment!" I could sense that she couldn't have cared less whether we'd taken the stairs or the lift, and as we walked side by side that afternoon through the series of elaborately decorated rooms, we did so just as any other couple would.

She hadn't once awkwardly glanced at the wheelchair beneath me and she had a clear disregard for its importance in what defined me as a person.

Hours had passed by in the blink of an eye. Not even the cold, November chill could deter us from exploring every inch of the castle grounds. All too soon, it was time for us both to head home. I offered to walk TJ back to her car, but she protested as she'd parked at the bottom of a hill. Undeterred, I said that I didn't mind (at this stage relatively confident that the date had gone so well that I might get a kiss as we said goodbye). Eventually, having walked down a long winding slope to where she had parked, we said our goodbyes. She leant down toward me with her arms outstretched. This was the first kiss moment (in my eyes at least). She hugged me tightly and said, "It's been so lovely to see you again. I look forward to doing this again!" But there was no kiss as I'd hoped to reward the long, slow climb back to where my car was parked. Regardless, I pushed back up the hill bursting with confidence that the date had gone so well – kiss or no kiss.

The more TJ and I talked, and the more we continued with our early form of what would blossom into a long-distance relationship, I could sense that I was working through some of the emotional insecurities and vulnerabilities that had plagued any chance of romantic happiness in the years since my accident. My foremost fear had been that a partner may come to resent the fact that I was in a wheelchair, and that I'd have my heart broken again. But nothing seemed to phase TJ. On our third date, this time in Oxford, I adamantly asserted that I could manage a large step into a country pub without any help. Seconds later I found myself flying backwards out of my wheelchair and into a stinking pile of fresh horse poo that had been conveniently left to break my fall. Working as a team, we managed to scrape off the larger clumps of manure, get me back into my chair and still laugh about "poo-gate" over dinner.

One adventure led to another, whether that was rambling over the rolling Shropshire hills, travelling to the pristine lakes of North Wales or exploring the forests of Hampshire. With each escapade, our connection would grow stronger, and the potential hardship of making a long-distance relationship work grew simpler. But then came the real test – inviting TJ to spend the weekend at home with me in Shrewsbury, and introducing her to my roommate, Nan. Suffice to say, Nan was elated that I was managing to move on from the heartbreak that she'd seen me struggle with since the day I moved in with her. There were two things that TJ would come to learn quickly about life at Nan's. First off, Nan's hearing was dreadfully unreliable. If what you were saying was important, it was often worth reciting twice. Second, and as I'd come to take for granted, "Fancy a cup of tea love?" would become a familiar call from her throughout the day. There was also something we'd learn together very quickly… Nan wouldn't knock before bursting into the bedroom!

In centuries of old, sailors had used the North Star as a navigational tool. The bright, shining way finder sat against the darkness of the night's sky and gave them hope of safe passage. And yet, it was in the moment when I was surrounded by darkness, my vision shrouded by fear and self-doubt, that TJ would enter my life and show me the path to true happiness. She saw something in me I thought I'd already lost.

15

BACK TO THE MOUNTAINS

There was a satisfying crunch as my skis glided effortlessly across the packed snow. God, I'd missed that sound. It evoked memories of days spent in the mountains, the solid crack of my winter boots on the ground beneath my feet, the endless possibility for the adventure ahead – a total, unbound connection to nature. For three years, I had stubbornly searched for ways in which I could replicate the visceral feeling of a day spent in the mountains, the natural high of conquering the terrain ahead of me. Now, as I glided across the pristine, snow-covered Norwegian wilderness, it occurred to me that I might have just recaptured the very thing that had eluded me since my life so abruptly changed.

It was a crisp -5°C in Rondane National Park, Norway, approximately 300km north of Oslo. I was part of a 12-strong contingent representing the Armed Forces Para-Snowsport Team (AFPST), a charity dedicated to helping injured and sick military personnel discover the transformative power of snowsports. Whilst fate had ultimately curtailed my service within the Army Reserve and had ended my dream of serving as part of the SAS Reserve, the military family would continue to support me on my journey of self-discovery. It was thanks to their support that I had been given the incredible opportunity to travel to Norway and to understand the uninhibited freedom afforded by a cross-country – or Nordic – sit-ski.

I'd flown from Birmingham with a small group of those whom I would come to ski with over the coming week, including Luke Wigman, a soldier in the RAF Regiment who stood on an IED in Afghanistan. During the flight, we traded stories of our injuries and rehabilitations, as well as our hopes and aspirations for the future. What Luke modestly described as a passion for "a bit of running," later transpired to be a thirst for ultra-endurance running, including having run seven marathons in seven days over seven continents – twice! An easy, natural friendship began to form between the two of us. It took no time at all to start joking at each other's expense, Luke brandishing me "such a diva" to the flight crew as I was carried onto the plane, my justified retaliation being to hide his passport as he attempted to board the plane behind me. Humour and mischief are the pillars of every great friendship.

We were greeted at Oslo Airport by the cheerful smile of Elizabeth Winfield, Liz, the charity's Chief Executive. I'd first met Liz at a newcomers' event held by the charity at the Tamworth Snowdome and before I knew it, she was excitedly talking about how Nordic skiing could help me to reconnect with my roots. "You'll be back in the mountains before you know it," she said enthusiastically. Three months later, Liz was driving the AFPST van through the darkness as we headed for the distant Norwegian wilderness. With little ambient light on our arrival, except for the crystal-clear twinkling stars above, it wouldn't be until morning that we came to appreciate the unspoilt beauty of the landscape in which we found ourselves.

Gathering around the long oak table at the centre of our accommodation the next morning, Liz stood proudly at the head of the table and welcomed us to the first day of our weeklong Nordic training camp. Not all of us would be learning to use a sit-ski; there would be some, like Luke, who would learn to cross-country ski in the traditional sense. I was to be part of a group of four and would be coached by Liz and Carl Simmons, one of the volunteer instructors for AFPST. The beauty of our lodge was that, once we opened the front door, we were straight onto the snow. On that first morning, I excitedly swung open the front door, inhaled a deep breath of crisp mountain air, and pushed myself out into the snow still sitting in my wheelchair. Suffice it to say, I made it no more than a foot from the door before getting stuck. I was going nowhere, but in a sit-ski I would leave my wheelchair far behind.

Liz and Carl briefed us on the fundamentals of how we would use a sit-ski (also known as a "rig"), which looked something like a raised bucket seat with two skis strapped beneath it. We would use two ski poles with spikes at their base to propel ourselves forward. Once on the snow and strapped into my rig, I intuitively dug my poles into the snow and pushed them backwards. I glided fluidly and seemingly effortlessly away from my wheelchair. With each push, I got further and further from our snow-topped accommodation. New snow crunched beneath my skis. The immediate sense of freedom and independence was, quite simply, immense. Carl shouted across to me, "Hold on Darren, I haven't got my skis on yet!" I was eager to start my first great adventure on snow since 2015!

I'd been guilty of thinking that, unlike learning to kayak, there wouldn't be any risk of falling over (repeatedly) as part of learning the Nordic sit-ski process. I was sadly mistaken! The backcountry routes surrounding our accommodation were under two feet of snow, save for the ski tracks carved by those powering off ahead of us. As I rounded a bend that sloped away to my right-hand side, the skis started to skid from beneath me – and I didn't have a clue how to effectively control the slide. This was starting to feel like a one-way ticket to my first capsize on snow. Liz jumped into action from behind, skiing over to my right-hand-side to act as a buffer between me and a pile of powder-fresh snow. I started to tip over toward Liz – and there was no amount of flailing ski poles that could stop the inevitable. I knocked Liz over, and then moments later fell on top of her, burying her in the snow just a bit deeper for good measure. We burst out into fits of laughter as we brushed the snow from our faces. Carl stood laughing above us as he reached for his phone to take a picture before helping to heave us out of the snowdrift.

To say that I was anything less than "consistent" across the first two days of my introduction to Nordic skiing would be highly inaccurate. I would start slowly, tentatively pushing myself across the snow to begin with, before gaining a little too much confidence close to a bend, at which point I'd need to be fished out of the snow. The problem was, I loved the exhilarating sense of speed and adrenaline as I worked the sit-ski hard across the snow. To traverse a landscape otherwise inaccessible by wheelchair and to be in the mountains once more moving under my own power was nothing short of magical.

On our third day in Norway, we travelled to Lillehammer, the home of the 1994 Winter Olympics, and which also happened to be hosting the 2019 Para-Nordic World Championships that very day. Luke and I walked along the perimeter of the 5km racetrack as we watched athletes from various countries warming up in front of us. We were joined by another member of our group, Jonny Huntington. Jonny's story was one to which all that Luke and I could say in unison was, "Fair play, mate." His journey had started five years prior, when having recently commissioned as an Officer in the British Army, he was struck down by a brain bleed that would leave him paralysed down the left side of his body. He had spent every moment since that fateful day learning to walk again, even if by his jovial description, "I still walk like I've had a few too many G&Ts." There was something about spending time with individuals like Luke and Jonny, individuals who epitomised the three words "strength through adversity" that led to an easy, natural connection forged through shared hardship.

There was a surprise in store. Having cheered on from the side-lines as we watched the GB Para-Nordic team compete at the World Championships, thanks to Liz's connections, the next day we were about to experience what it was like to race on the World Cup course for ourselves. Better still, representatives from GB Snowsport would be there to watch us. There was one overriding thought in my head: "Just don't make a tit out of yourself, Darren." Arriving at the venue, our group hurried about sorting kit and equipment, eager to get out on the immaculate snow track ahead of us. I would be part of a small group of sit-ski athletes alongside two members of the group I'd enjoyed getting to know – Steve and Bryan. It wasn't too long before we found ourselves at the start line, ready to beast ourselves around the track.

I was off. My poles dug into the compact snow as I propelled myself along the 100m straight ahead of me. There was a gradual climb up a short, sharp hill in front of me. Liz was behind me, shouting instructions like a rally co-pilot as I had to drive down harder to maintain any momentum up the climb. "Pole, pole, pole!" came the call from Liz. Slowly, I began to crest the top of the hill. Reaching the top of the manmade mound, I caught the first glimpse of what was on the other side – a steep decline leading to a hairpin left turn (with an ominous 10ft drop off to the immediate right). A bit like those first few moments of ominous regret after jumping on a scary rollercoaster ride for the first time, before I knew it, I was sliding down towards the drop ahead of me. “Left Darren, more left Darren!” came Liz’s cry from behind. I was confident I could turn it in on time. My plan was simply to swing my hips beneath me at the last moment and I’d carve out an epic handbrake turn. Importantly, I’d forgotten one key piece of information. I can’t move my hips! With the perilous drop now right ahead of me, there was only one option left – bail! I leaned as far left as I could, digging my poles into the snow as if they were ice axes, and with Liz speeding up and grabbing the back of the sit-ski, we averted what had felt like the inevitable. Once more, we lay in the snow, Liz laughing as she was pinned beneath my ski rig before Carl appeared again with his phone at the ready.

My week in Norway soon drew to a close and as we made our way back to Oslo airport ready to fly home, I knew that although it had taken three years for me to rediscover the visceral magic the mountains possess, it wouldn’t be another three before I’d return. Just as importantly, the trip had also been an opportunity to forge friendships with those with whom I shared so much in common. So many elements of my story were reflected in theirs: adversity, struggle, heartbreak and triumph. It had been an honour to meet Carl, Luke and Jonny, but fate told me that our futures would in some way be intertwined.

16

FACING FAILURE

The seasons had come and gone at the National Water Sports Centre, but my goal had doggedly remained the same – to race at the Paralympic Games in Tokyo. In the world of elite sport, no one's place is guaranteed; change is eternal. I'd had to say an emotional farewell to both Jen and Will, who had departed Nottingham for pastures new. I was now surrounded by a new collection of faces, each of us chasing the elusive dream of competing internationally alongside our teammates in the senior squad. The security of my position within the programme was by no means a foregone conclusion and it certainly hadn't been without its challenges. But with determination and grit, I managed to keep my place secure.

I drifted forward, letting my boat float into the starting gate in Lane 7, seconds from the first race of the season. In the lane to the left was my training partner and main competitor, Stewart Clarke. We were about to race in a type of kayak known as a Va'a, which would be making its debut at the 2020 Paralympics in Tokyo. The Va'a was used extensively throughout the Pacific Ocean for more than 4,000 years and has been successfully adopted by the world of sprint canoeing. Athletes paddle fast and furiously on one side of their boat, with an outrigger floating off the same side, beyond the reach of their canoe paddle. I'd made the switch across to the Va'a six months previously, under the guidance of my coach Roger Weir, and it was my best chance of achieving my goals for the pivotal year ahead. The sound of the loudspeaker cut through the silence over the water: "Starters take your positions." I leant forward into the strap across my torso, my paddle outstretched, ready to drive down and through the water. I was a coiled spring, ready to leap into action.

Each competitor was poised, waiting for the distinctive third loud beep from the race controller. The speaker attached to my starting gate beeped twice, and then for a third and final time as the bucket holding the nose of my Va'a dropped into the water. I speared the water with my paddle, driving down powerfully in a series of short and sharp strokes as I built momentum off the start line. In my peripheral vision, I could see the spray of water coming off Stewart's paddle as he exploded off the line beside me. A quarter of the way in, with 175 metres to go, we were neck and neck. The crowds along the water grew in number as we headed toward the finish line, their fervent cheers of encouragement secondary to the sound of our boats accelerating through the water. I began to lengthen my strokes, putting more power through the blade as I reached top speed. Stewart was now half a boat length ahead of me, but I was still within touching distance with just 75 metres left.

Fatigue was starting to creep in. I could feel the lactic acid in the muscles of my arms building, but I knew that I was on course for a time that would qualify me to race at the next World Championships. "Come on Darren, only 50 metres to go!" I thought to myself, gritting my teeth. Yet, as I leaned forward to take my next stroke, I found myself unexpectedly falling forward toward the rim of my cockpit. I instinctively let one hand go from my paddle to stop my head from hitting the top of the boat. What on earth had just happened? Looking down, I saw that the strap around my torso was hanging loosely from my seat, not helping to hold me in position at all. I tried to take another stroke but fell forward once more. The backrest of my seat had broken away from the base of my boat. I glanced across in desperation to the side of the lake for my coach as others began to overtake me, and as my dream of posting an international qualifying time now lay in tatters. I limped across the line 15 seconds after my target time. My frustrations boiled over as I slammed the paddle against the outrigger.

Stewart had finished more than ten seconds ahead of me and had already spun his boat around, expecting to see me on his shoulder. He waited on the water for me to drag my broken boat across the finish line, before taking a few strokes in my direction. "What on earth happened, Darren? I thought you were right on top of me?!" he enquired with a degree of surprise to his voice.

"My backrest snapped with 50 metres to go," I replied, unable to keep the disappointment from my voice. Stewart leant over and put his arm around my shoulders. "Next time, mate. Keep your head up," he said in a conciliatory tone. As well as a fiercely competitive athlete, Stewart was also incredibly genuine in how he wanted to see me progress – and challenge him. In a sport where, ultimately, only one of us might go on to represent Great Britain at the Paralympics, Stewart's selflessness spoke volumes about his character. Not performing to my expectations was a bitter pill for us both to swallow.

However, there was a more pressing issue to address than a broken seat, and it would take more than a quick fix in a workshop to rectify the situation. It was something that, in all honesty, meant my future at British Canoeing hung in the balance. For more than three months, I had been training through levels of pain I'd not experienced before. The rigorous physical demands that success called for were causing agony in my left shoulder. As weeks and months ticked by, the pain had become almost omnipotent in every aspect of my daily life and began to have a significant impact on my mental well-being. I became fearful of disclosing details of the injury to the coaches or athletes at Nottingham, as I knew that it would undoubtedly have its implications for the pivotal 12 months ahead. The unwelcome truth was that I'd partially torn the rotator cuff in my left shoulder, which attaches the humerus (upper arm bone) to the shoulder blade. The instructions from a private physio were simple: "This is only going to get worse if you carry on down this path. You need to rest and rehabilitate your shoulder properly."

It was time. I couldn't hide or disguise my struggle with injury any longer. Arriving at Nottingham on a rainy Monday morning not long after the British Championship, I found Roger down in the boat bay waiting to start our first training session of the week – sets of 100-metre sprints up and down the lake. "Could we talk?" I asked gingerly.

"That's what we always tend to do before a session, isn't it?" came Roger's joking response.

I intimated that it was a bit more of a serious conversation than our usual Monday morning banter, so with that in mind, we headed up to one of the conference rooms in the main British Canoeing building. Over the course of the next 30 minutes, I came clean about the extent to which I'd struggled with my injury, how I was so determined to push through regardless, but that it was now having an impact on my ability to simply push a wheelchair around. Something had to change.

Roger's response only validated the reason for us having the conversation: "Darren, I can see that you've been struggling – it's hard not to notice the way you've been rolling and rubbing your shoulder between sets – but I decided to leave it in your court to tell me if it's a serious issue." A wave of embarrassment washed over me. Why had I been so scared to admit the truth? "Look," Roger continued, "you should have told me. But I know that you've been so determined to chase your dream of qualifying for Tokyo. Let's put a plan together that gives you the best chance of rehabilitating in time, but you need to know that there are no guarantees with this kind of thing," he said resolutely. Only time would tell.

The uncertainty of my future at Nottingham aside, I was entering a period of change and growth at home. I was about to take a significant step forward in my rehabilitation journey – living on my own for the first time since leaving the hospital three years ago. My time living at Nan's had sadly come to an end. It was time to prove to myself, and to all those who loved me, that I could not just survive living on my own but thrive. No longer would I hear the ever-tempting call of, "Fancy a cup of tea love?" from down the stairwell, no more late-night chats about life and no more comfort in knowing that there was always Nan on-hand if I needed help with something.

The day I picked up the keys to my new home was as exciting as it was sad. It was the end of a chapter. A chapter that I'd enjoyed more than I ever could have appreciated when it first began. As I left Nan's for the final time, we embraced tightly on the doorstep, an unspoken admission that we'd miss each other dearly hanging in the air between us. Holding back tears, Nan looked at me and said, "It's been one of the happiest times of my life having you here."

"Me too, Nan. Me too," came my heartfelt response.

17

STEPPING STONE

What is a failure if it is not a stepping stone to future success? All too often we harbour self-limiting beliefs that have a direct influence over what we achieve. Of course, sometimes we do fail. We might strive toward an aspirational goal for more than three years, simply to see it slip through our fingers. But does that mean we should avoid risking failure at all costs? Absolutely not! For it is striving toward a goal that gives us a sense of direction, purpose and passion in life. Even if we fall short, what is to say that beyond failure doesn't lie the greatest achievement of our lives?

I couldn't remember the last time I'd stated a clear goal, or a well-defined statement of purpose, only to fail to see it come to fruition. I feared failure. The problem was, I was now staring at the ever-increasing probability that this would be the logical conclusion of my dream to represent Great Britain at the Paralympics. I fought against the temptation to quit before someone else could fail me, just like I had seen countless soldiers admit defeat over the mountains of the Brecon Beacons during Selection. The allure of an immediate end to physical suffering had been too strong for them. Physically, I was hurting, even after we drastically scaled back my training workload to the bare minimum. Psychologically, I was so emotionally invested that I feared failure might significantly impact my mental health. However, fate was about to cast its deciding vote.

It was a cool, Easter afternoon on the water. I'd just finished a long, slow paddle along the beautiful Montgomery Canal in Shropshire. The sounds and colours of spring surrounded me as I drifted back to the boathouse alongside my good friend and training partner, Lauren Homewood. It had been six months since I'd confided in Roger about my injury, and it was thanks to Lauren and her family that I'd been able to get out on the water while the emphasis of my training had been on rehabilitating my damaged rotator cuff – even if we were limited to one or two relaxed outings a week. However, the world had irreversibly changed since my conversation with Roger. There were growing murmurs in the press that the UK might be headed into a state of national lockdown. The Covid-19 pandemic had swept across the globe: first the initial outbreak in China, then chaos and confusion as the death toll climbed in Italy, and now the UK was seemingly locked in its sights as the next epicentre of the virus.

"What days are you free to train next week?" I asked Lauren as she brought my wheelchair trundling along the towpath toward me.

"I guess it depends on what Boris has to say tonight doesn't it?" she responded with an air of the inevitable in her voice.

It was 23 March 2020. There was no way we could have known it at that moment, but it would be our last training session together until late June, a little over three months later. No one could have anticipated the scale at which the UK would be hit by Covid or the extent to which it would permeate every aspect of society – including the world of elite sports competition. Sitting on the banks of the canal that afternoon, my only hope was for more days of uninterrupted training as I looked to build myself back up, stronger than ever before.

On 24 March 2020, the International Olympic Committee announced that the Olympiad in Tokyo would be moved to 2021 due to the developing global pandemic – although several high-profile sources cast doubt, believing that even a 12-month delay was overly optimistic. In the weeks that followed the announcement by the IOC, and as my hopes and dreams hung by a thread, flooded in the sea of global volatility, I thought back to how it felt to be on bed rest during those six weeks in hospital – life seemingly out of my control, simply a passenger pulled along by the prevailing winds. I remembered how liberating it had felt to find the elements that I could control: my mindset, my spirometer, my ability to plan for the future. Even these small acts helped to create certainty from uncertainty. Perhaps that is what I needed now more than ever. There was no guarantee that the Paralympic Games would go ahead, even in 2021, and there was no guarantee that my shoulder would recover quick enough to give me a shot at qualifying. Maybe it was time to tread my own path, one that I would ultimately be accountable for forging despite any and all adversity.

I sat at the small table in my living room, my laptop and notebook cramped onto one half of it. TJ was sitting across from me, midway through teaching her Year 4 class via Microsoft Teams, with her whiteboard and assortment of pens strewn across the other half of the table. The announcement of the UK's first lockdown had, as for many couples, accelerated the pace at which our relationship was moving. It was a natural progression for us and living together was certainly a welcome relief from the challenges of making a long-distance relationship work. However, there was one battleground upon which we would fight for every inch possible – space at the living room table. We'd both developed skills and tactics to covertly encroach over each other's side of the border. It was against the backdrop of Year 4's latest mathematics lesson, as I stared at a map of the United Kingdom, that I was suddenly struck by a moment of pure curiosity. Would it be possible to kayak from Land's End to John O' Groats? Specifically, would it be possible for someone with a disability to take on this iconic challenge?

The idea took hold in my mind and spread like wildfire. From what I could see, it had only been done twice before, and by two able-bodied kayakers. Both crossings had taken more than 30 days as they travelled over 1,400 kilometres across the high seas, vast lochs and meandering rivers of the British Isles. As soon as TJ had wrapped up her virtual lesson, I excitedly said five words that she had come accustomed to hearing throughout the course of our relationship, "I've had a brilliant idea!"

She laughed, before replying, "Go on, let's hear it then…"

I told her about my fledgling idea to prove exactly what individuals with a disability could achieve, to which she simply responded, "Why not!" It was exactly the response I'd wanted and needed to hear, and I think she knew that. Emboldened by her unconditional support, and with the bit now firmly between my teeth, ready to turn this crazy dream into reality, I ordered a copy of *Sea Kayaking* to improve my understanding of the challenges and pitfalls of what lay ahead: tidal patterns, tidal races, sea states, wind, navigation. I also knew exactly who I wanted to be part of this incredible endeavour with me.

It was the third week of the UK's national lockdown. I was back at the dinner table once more, but this time waiting patiently for my Zoom call to start, and for it to begin populating with the faces I knew would soon be joining. First popped up the familiar face of Jonny Huntington, then Carl Simmons, both of whom I had met in Norway a year earlier. Now we were only waiting for one final person to join… Luke Wigman. Everyone knew what we were there to discuss because they'd all said yes, without much persuasion, to being part of what could become a historic "World First" by an adaptive team. It was so great to see everyone together again, albeit virtually. I'd been eagerly prepping for this first meeting for over a week, and I was keen to show the lads that I'd been doing my homework – or at least that I'd read my copy of *Sea Kayaking* from front to back, alongside practising some basic navigation and expedition planning exercises.

The meeting started on something of a comical note. As we all already knew each other, we recognised that we shared the same grit, determination and resilience to be able to achieve a goal. However, what we didn't know was anything about each other's level of previous kayaking experience. Jonny started us off in an almost apologetic tone, saying, "To be honest lads, I've not done all that much out at sea, maybe like one or two small forays into a bay – that's about it." I joked that Jonny's "two small forays" at sea made him 100 percent more seaworthy than me – someone who had spent three years sprinting up and down the same lake! Thankfully, Carl's career as a PTI in the British Army had allowed him to specialise in adventurous training activities, which included kayaking. Finally, it was Luke's turn to reveal the true depths of his experience at sea.

"Right lads," he began. "When I said yes to this challenge, I did so knowing that the only time I've been in a kayak was on my honeymoon in Cancun for 20 minutes maximum. That's it!" The group burst out into laughter as Luke protested, "I only wish I was bloody joking," through fits of laughter.

We were a band of misfits with no real right to be attempting to take on a challenge of this magnitude, but as Jonny said as the meeting ended: "It's all within the art of the possible!"

What was clear from the outset was that we wanted our challenge to have a purpose, to do more than to show the world what individuals with life-changing injuries could achieve, but to also raise a target of £100,000 for charity. It was immediately clear to the team which charity that would be – the Armed Forces Para-Snowsport Team, the charity through which we all had the opportunity to meet. We approached Liz Winfield, the charity's CEO, and she was instantly excited and utterly committed to making this happen. Her boundless energy became a real asset to the group as we forged forward with our planning and branding. "Kayak 4 Heroes" was officially announced to the world in May 2020, with plans in place for our first team training day as soon as lockdown rules permitted.

Three months had passed since our inaugural meeting on Zoom and it had been a catalyst for more virtual planning sessions as we began to develop our ever-evolving solution to how we would overcome this unproven, challenging expedition. But today was an important milestone in our Kayak 4 Heroes journey because I was headed south to meet the team at the Cotswold Water Park for our first physical training session. Early July had been our first possible opportunity to come together once lockdown restrictions began to ease.

Typically, we'd been blessed with typically British summer weather – wet and windy! Once everyone arrived and the banter was flowing, we started to transfer our paddling kit down to the lakeside in between torrential downpours. Jonny and I had brought our own kayaks, so Liz, in her newly created and highly prestigious role as "Operations Manager" for our expedition, sourced two rather weather-beaten snub-nosed kayaks for Luke and Carl to use. As we huddled beneath the boot lid of my car for a momentary reprieve from the lashing rain, Luke looked out over the windswept lake and made a profound observation: "I won't lie, this looks a little different to Cancun!"

Fortunately, each of us were proponents of the theory: "If it isn't raining, it isn't training". Undeterred, we set off across the lake on our maiden voyage. The small, man-made lake was the perfect training ground for us to start building our confidence on the water. Jonny had arrived with a super sleek-looking kayak, and it cut effortlessly through the water as he led the way ahead of Carl and me, who paddled side by side. As we slowly paddled along the shoreline of the lake, we expected to hear Luke catching up from behind us, but he wasn't to be seen or heard. It was only once we'd spun to face the pontoon from which we'd departed that we saw Luke unintentionally spinning on the spot as he tried but failed to paddle in any one direction. "It'll take a long time to paddle to John O' Groats if you do it in circles!" Carl shouted as he doubled back to help rescue Luke from his dizzying predicament.

For the next two hours, we performed loops along the perimeter of the lake, which allowed me to chat informally on a one-to-one basis with the team. What was interesting was how the guys perceived different aspects of our expedition as posing the greatest challenge. For some, it was the physical attrition on the body of kayaking day in and day out for over a month. For others, it was how we would need to mitigate the risk of serious injury (or worse). What each conversation shared, though, was a solution-focussed approach to the obstacles ahead of us – adapt, improvise and overcome. As we approached the end of our first foray together, we made our way across to the pontoon, where Liz had been joined by a friend of mine who also happened to be a professional photographer, Josh Raper. We huddled side by side as we paused for Josh to take a picture of us with our paddles raised proudly in the air. We'd made it across the first, albeit very modest, stepping stone of our journey ahead. It was time to step up the intensity of our training!

18

ONE BREATH

Scrolling through my Instagram feed one afternoon, I came across a video of a man diving beneath the water along the wreckage of a sixteenth-century Spanish galleon. He was surrounded by shades of sapphire blue and turquoise, the water full of vivid colour. His movements were composed, fluid and highly efficient. He looked unbound by the laws of physics. There were no signs of an oxygen tank or a respirator and as the video continued it was impossible to imagine being able to hold my breath for so long. Searching through the post's description, and then through the man's bio, it appeared that he was something known as a "freediver". I rewatched the video, this time paying close attention to how he turned and twisted his body gracefully underwater. At that moment, I realised what I had been searching for since becoming paralysed – the ability to move my entire body uninhibited, away from the confines of a seated position. I had just found out how I might be able to achieve it.

Having reached out to a company called Go Freediving, based at Vobster Quay in the southwest of England, I spoke on the phone with Emma Farrell, one of the world's leading freediving instructors. When I asked if she thought it would be possible for me to learn to dive, irrespective of my injury, her encouraging response was, "100 percent yes. With absolute certainty. Nothing is stopping you." Emma and her team were beginning to tentatively open their business again after the first wave of the pandemic had shut everything down, and I'd just secured myself a slot at their upcoming introduction to freediving course.

The mist of a cold October morning was suspended above the ice-blue water in front of me. From where I sat, it looked as if time had stood still here. A millennium may have elapsed around it, but the lake looked untouched by the hand of time. As I braced myself for the cold embrace of the water, I revelled in the excitement of finding a new way to connect back to nature and hopefully rediscover this element that had been missing from my life since Matt had saved my life at World's End. The warmth of my wetsuit protected me from the crisp, autumnal air. I put my arms up and around the shoulders of Emma and Mark as they lifted me out of my chair and proceeded to carry me across broken ground to the water's edge. It was time to freedive.

I could feel the lake's cold embrace as water began to seep through the small gaps in my neoprene hood before flooding down into my suit. I floated effortlessly on the surface of the water, the buoyancy of the freediving wetsuit giving me a feeling of weightlessness. Emma pointed to an orange marker buoy about 10 metres in the distance. "Will you be okay to swim over there, or do you need help?" she asked.

"Are you kidding? I was counting on a swim to warm up a bit," I joked. I swam the short distance to the buoy using front crawl, trying to keep pace with Emma's effortless finning. Beneath the floating orange marker, a rope line was secured to the wreckage of a sailing boat 10 metres below.

I tilted my head into the water, peering into the depths,

trying to find any sign of what was beneath us. The rope simply disappeared into the darkness. Emma began to talk me through the process of how I would need to "breathe up" before committing to each dive. The key was to enter as relaxed a state as possible, allowing the lungs and diaphragm to empty of carbon dioxide and then flood with oxygen. "The most important bit to remember is that this is all to do with remaining calm underwater – control your thoughts, stay calm, don't waste oxygen by beginning to panic," Emma said evenly.

My right hand tightly held the top of the rope tied beneath the buoy. I steadied my breathing, fully immersing myself in how it felt to empty and refill my lungs. With one last, long inhale, I pulled with my right hand to fully immerse myself underwater. I reached down with my left hand to the rope below, grasping it and pulling myself deeper still. With each alternating pull, my body descended further into the looming darkness. The pressure of the water continued to build. I paused for a moment to pinch my nose and equalise my ears before continuing to pull deeper once more. Surely, I must be close to reaching the bottom of the line by now? Slowly, the outline of a boat began to emerge from obscurity. But doubt started to creep into my mind. If I descended any further, would I have enough oxygen to make it back to the surface? At that moment, self-doubt overwhelmed my fragile confidence. I turned to pull on the rope above, letting it run through my fingers as I rose buoyantly to the surface.

"That was incredible!" Emma exclaimed as she put her arm underneath mine while I steadied my breath. "That was one hell of a first dive," she continued, "and I could tell that you could have kept going. Just have faith in your breath-hold ability." She was right. It was only once I'd breached the surface of the water that I realised I still had spare oxygen in the tank.

"I'm getting down to the boat next time," I declared confidently, as I began to slow my breathing in preparation to descend into the dark once more. This time I pulled harder on the rope, lengthening the distance between each grasp as my body continued efficiently on its downward vertical voyage. The boat was soon within touching distance. With one last pull, I let go of the rope. My body's momentum carried me easily to the roof of the boat's cabin. I hung for a moment, suspended effortlessly in the water. Reaching my hands out in front of me, I scooped the water in my hands, performing an underwater breaststroke. Like a dolphin frolicking in its boundless ability, I excitedly experimented with how effortlessly I could move my entire body through the water – no longer eternally stuck in a seated position, experiencing only the unparalleled freedom of fluid expression. It was only once the levels of carbon dioxide began to climb in my system that I was reminded my natural existence was on the surface.

Gathering my breath for a moment, I was overcome by the visceral sense of freedom I'd felt beneath the water. I looked Emma in the eyes, and said, "I can't tell you how special that was. Honestly, I can't find the words to accurately express how it felt."

She leant forward in the water to embrace me. "It was beautiful to see you playing around down there, moving your body so fluidly with just your hands."

It's funny, it hadn't felt that long since I was at the spinal unit struggling to lift the first Ping-Pong ball of my spirometer, my lungs too weak to inhale any serious volume of oxygen. Now, they were the tool that would allow me to submerge myself into a different reality, a reality within which my disability faded to insignificance. There was only one question in Emma's mind. "Fancy going deeper and doing something cool?" she teased, with a glint in her eye.

I descended slowly into the darkness, deeper than before. Suddenly, the temperature of the water noticeably dropped. I'd hit what is known as a "thermocline", a thin but distinct line at which water temperatures drop at depth. From the murky depths emerged the outline of a large military aircraft, what looked like a Douglas C-47. As I reached the mid-section of the aircraft, 12 metres below the surface, I peered through the broken fuselage of the plane. There was a clear path through the mid-section to the other side of the plane; swimming through it was my target. But I doubted myself. The seconds continued to tick by. 40 seconds, 41 seconds, 42 seconds. The longer I waited, holding the edge of the fuselage, the less oxygen I would have to make the swim. Emma and Mark shadowed me, keeping a close eye on my movements. I couldn't do it on this attempt, I told myself, what if I started to struggle for oxygen halfway through? Once I'd surrendered to self-doubt there was no turning back. I headed for the surface.

Something profound occurred to me. What I once loved about climbing was how it tested my psychological strength, my ability to remain calm in moments of elevated risk, and my confidence in the mastery of my instincts and senses. It was these exact elements of psychological testing that I was experiencing again for the first time since my injury. I had to master the skill of remaining calm underwater, trusting my instincts and committing myself to gradually pushing the envelope of what I believed to be possible. I turned to Mark, and with renewed confidence said, "This time I'm going all the way through!"

"I love the confidence," came his reply.

I took the time to perform a proper, slow breathe up. My body entering a state of total relaxation. At that moment, all that I was aware of was the gentle rise and fall of my ribcage as I breathed deeply. My grip tightened around the rope in my left hand as I began my dive. I reached each hand out in turn as I pulled down the line, only pausing occasionally to equalise the pressure in my ears. The dive clock had passed 20 seconds by the time I reached the plane 12 metres down. I fluidly moved my body into position so that I could see through the broken fuselage. I committed without hesitation this time. My arms propelled me forward as my body entered the rusted surroundings of the plane's interior. The dive clock hit 35 seconds as I emerged from the opposite end. I glanced fleetingly to the surface of the water above me, before looking determinedly back through the plane. My emotions were under control, my instinct telling me that I had enough oxygen to swim back through the plane. I manipulated the position of my body as I began the return leg of my swim. By the time I emerged on the other side to start my ascent, I'd been underwater for 45 seconds. My chest started to tighten as the levels of carbon dioxide in my system began to rise. In the weirdest way, as I was fighting to control the self-doubt and panic from rising, I hadn't felt more alive in the longest time. I'd emerged from the darkness and into the light.

19

GETTING SERIOUS

When the Kayak 4 Heroes team announced to the world its intention to kayak 1,400 kilometres from Land's End to John O' Groats, tackling some of the toughest and most dangerous coastal waters in Europe, not many people believed that it could be done. Not that it couldn't be physically done, but because they didn't think that we, our team, could do it. In particular, people failed to believe that someone with a high-level spinal cord injury could make the journey successfully. One person even went as far as to single me out as "the weak link" in the team. I was acutely aware that there was no guarantee of success – far from it. But I was equally aware that if I failed to venture forth, then there was categorically no way that I would ever know if we could achieve the impossible. Sometimes you must go against the grain and use other people's doubts to fuel your own success.

After announcing the expedition, we had 12 months before we would set off beneath the jagged cliffs of Land's End, where the Atlantic Ocean first strikes the Cornish coastline. Preparations started in earnest. A key pillar of our methodology was coming together twice a month as a team for a weekend-long training camp, giving us the opportunity to practice parts of the route we would be taking in June 2021. Having successfully survived the strikingly calm waters of the Cotswold Water Park in July, a month later we moved on to a stretch of the River Severn that would form part of the 350-kilometre inland section of our expedition. Thankfully, Luke had proved himself more than capable of paddling in a straight line – and was no longer openly professing his hatred for kayaking! The motto "adapt, improvise and overcome" perfectly captured how we would solve the ever-evolving puzzle of achieving a true world-first, defying all odds and expectations.

It was October 2020, and I was about to achieve a major milestone in my rehabilitation journey. Once again, I found myself cradled in the arms of two conveniently strong friends. This time I wasn't being passed over a gate post in Shropshire on the banks of the River Severn but being carried across the beach at Salcombe in Devon on my way to kayak at sea for the first time. "Daz, I hope you're going to be a bit lighter if you're expecting us to carry you every bloody day on the expedition," joked Jonny as he and Luke walked me to the water's edge. The turquoise sea twinkled beautifully in the bright autumnal sun. This was going to be the first big test of how my body would react to more challenging conditions. My excitement was palpable, my adrenaline pumping in nervous anticipation. In the water ahead of us waited Jim Taylor-Ross, the man who was fast becoming our official team coach and safety consultant. He was one of the most experienced coastal kayakers in the UK and had kindly offered his support, and that of his Epic brand of kayaks, in helping us to achieve our lofty ambition.

Jonny and Luke lowered me gently into the rear seat of Jim's double sea kayak and passed me my paddle. Before I knew it, we were carving our way effortlessly through the small waves as we headed out of the bay toward the horizon. I couldn't believe the speed and grace with which Jim paddled and I eagerly tried to imitate it to the best of my ability in the rear seat. With the imposing tree-topped cliffs of Salcombe to our right and open water to our left, we were joined by Jonny, Luke and Carl. The improvised backrest Jim had fashioned for me to sit against worked perfectly, and I found myself growing in confidence with each minute that passed. As a team, being out on open water together was an important milestone and confirmation that we weren't (at least not totally) crazy. In Jim's: "I think you're all a bit bonkers, but I believe that you can do it." It was all the validation we needed!

There was a genuine sense of camaraderie developing within the team as we pushed forward with our expedition preparations. As our story developed, people from across the UK began to connect with Kayak 4 Heroes via social media. We were inundated with offers of support, from people offering to open their homes as free accommodation, to those who simply wished to meet and cheer us along. One afternoon that October, I received a message on Instagram from Ben Gallagher, a soldier in the British Army who was in the process of being medically discharged after sustaining life-changing injuries in a near-fatal incident. He wanted to know if there were any opportunities to get involved or support our expedition. I instantly messaged the team on our shared WhatsApp to say that there might be an opportunity to involve Ben as a new member of our paddling team. After all, one of the purposes of our challenge was to prove exactly what could be achieved by individuals who had suffered life-changing injuries. Ben was at such a critical moment in his personal recovery story, and the team could see the potentially huge positive impact being part of our challenge could have for him. Commenting on Ben's good looks at our next Zoom meeting, Liz joked, "He could be our new poster boy!"

We were now a team of five determined and highly motivated would-be sea kayakers. With a healthy amount of joking and jesting at each other's expense, and with the invaluable support of Liz, Jim, and now Chris Powell and Ellie Cartwright from Wanderlust Action Films, who had offered their talents to tur our expedition into an uplifting documentary, there was a real sense of momentum building behind us. But, just as the impossible was beginning to feel within our grasp, the UK started experiencing a new wave of Covid. As daily infection figures began to rise through October, we feared the country was headed for a second national lockdown. On the 31 October, Boris Johnson stood behind his podium at 10 Downing Street to announce a new four-week national lockdown. There were now just seven months to go until our proposed start date, and with winter fast approaching, there was little confidence that the latest resurgence of the virus was going to subside any time soon.

In times of uncertainty, and when life feels seemingly out of our control, it is in these moments that we must focus on the elements within our lives that we can always take accountability for: our actions and our mindset. The UK wouldn't fully emerge from lockdown until after the chilly depths of winter had given way to new hope in the spring of 2021. For many onlookers, the months of lockdown and lack of training had surely washed away any last remnants of hope for our expedition. Yes, there were moments of doubt when I asked myself the hard question: are we running out of time to make this happen? And yet, the instinctive response of my mindset was always the same – adapt, improvise, overcome! Whilst the team couldn't physically meet and train, it didn't stop us from working as a virtual collective to address all the logistical factors that would be critical to the success of the expedition: route plan, navigation, support boat, land support crew, emergency procedures. Crucially, by focusing on the elements we could still control, we put ourselves in a positive position once the country emerged from lockdown. Far from defeated, we emerged more committed and determined to overcome adversity than ever before.

A WhatsApp message flashed up on my phone from Chris at Wanderlust Action Films. "Are you ready for a big sexy surprise?" I laughed at Chris's message, deliberately loaded with sexual innuendo.

"Stop teasing and show me the goods," came my toying response.

Without a second's delay, Chris sent through an image of something truly extraordinary: a big, military-style Rigid Inflatable Boat (RIB). It was the very thing we'd been looking for, and an element of our plan that had remained a vitally missing piece of our puzzle – a boat that could become our floating island and haven on the open oceans and wild seas!

"You can call me Captain Powell from now on, mate," came a follow-up message.

Without any pressure to do so, Chris used his experience to source (and purchase) the very boat he'd just sent the image of – and it looked like a beauty! Three powerful engines, space for all our safety and camera equipment, and even enough room for an occasional nautical nap on our way to and from our start and end points each day. It was perfect, and a game-changer in terms of the feasibility and potential success of our expedition.

There was still a lot of ground to cover, though, and we were running out of time. True to the cause, the team's valiant response to the challenges ahead was to graft harder, think smarter, and commit more of their personal time to make the expedition happen. Yet, there remained one big unanswered question upon which the success of our expedition depended: could we survive at sea and paddle over 50 kilometres each day?

We would find the answer on the gently cresting waves of the murky Bristol Channel, the second-largest tidal range in the world. As we exited through the harbour walls of Cardiff Bay aboard our new safety boat, under the command of "Captain Powell", I was eager to put our months of planning and training to the test. Chris's heavily laden RIB slowly left the confines of the harbour and the wide expanse of the Bristol Channel stood before us. Packed together like sardines, we readied our kit and prepared to drop our double sea kayaks into the water. This would be our first official sea trial and our aim was simple – to get 50 kilometres under our belts.

Through the months of intensive training in the build-up to setting sail on the Bristol Channel, which had taken us from locations in Devon, the Lake District and the River Severn, we habitually rotated the configuration of who paddled with who – and which pairings worked best and worst. Ben and I had found this out the hard way on a frost-bitten January morning as we capsized on our own along the icy waters of the River Severn, six or so kilometres away from our vehicles. By the time we'd rectified our situation and paddled back to the warmth of our cars, the water on our kayaking jackets had frozen solid. In fact, the only people I hadn't capsized with were Jonny and Jim. In truth, as we began to encounter more challenging conditions and sea states, and as I started to really test the limit of what I believed I was capable of, I gravitated toward Jim and Carl to help navigate me through troubled waters.

But today, as we dropped the first pairing of Jonny and Ben onto the slow, rolling waves of the Bristol Channel, I knew that, in these conditions, I could paddle with anybody. We would also be testing for the last time our system of rotating paddlers every 45 minutes – our own version of a waterborne relay race. We hoped that this approach would not only maximise our chances of success but would also help to keep the team as fresh as possible as we slowly worked our way up the length of Great Britain. One of the greatest challenges our team would face was how our individual injuries would leave us more vulnerable to serious injury. For me, it would be the risk of developing debilitating pressure sores made worse by the salty ocean water, or how I would cope with serious waves and swell as I fought to balance using only the muscles from my chest up. In Jonny's case, the lasting impacts of his neurological injury had become scarily apparent on our previous training weekend in North Devon. Caught out by increasing winds on an exposed headland, Jonny and Ben capsized and became submerged in the icy water for 20 minutes. By the time they'd be towed to safety by the heroics of Luke and Jim, Jonny's brain had begun to shut down his body, systematically and determinedly, bit by bit. I'd never seen him look so weak. This was going to be so much more than the simple act of five fit guys paddling from Land's End to John O' Groats, it would be a story of triumph over physical and psychological injuries.

For now, as we paddled merrily through the rhythmic, rolling waves of the Bristol Channel, and as we crunched kilometre after kilometre, confidence and morale couldn't have been higher. Chris, in one of his many responsibilities as our safety boat pilot, ensured that there was a constant stream of anthems emitting from the speakers aboard the RIB. But as I paddled toward the horizon with Carl with the iconic words of *Sweet Caroline* transmitting across the water, I couldn't help but fear that we were being lulled into a false sense of security. There were no cresting waves, no meaningful wind and the sun was shining brightly above. If only we could be sure of having days and moments like this on the expedition. We were now only a matter of weeks away from setting off from Land's End, and I felt like I was only just beginning to scratch the surface of what I was capable of.

That was all about to change.

20

IS THIS A JOKE?

I was surrounded by a beautiful pine forest. Sunlight poured through the canopy of the trees above and the pure, cleansing smell of the wilderness flooded my nostrils. Murphy, my young Border Collie, bounded playfully ahead as he chased a small branch. Despite the beauty of my surroundings, as TJ and I walked around the beautiful lake Llyn Alwe' in North Wales, I was visibly and emotionally on edge. This was a place of such happy memories for us as a couple, but as we began to ascend the gentle slope toward the highest point above the lake, I could feel my stomach turning as nerves began to bubble to the surface. I wasn't really talking much, and only uttered short responses to TJ's attempts at getting a conversation going; I was too absorbed in my own head, role-playing all the potentially different ways the next 10 minutes could unfold. TJ reached for her phone in the zip pocket in the back of my chair to take a picture, at which point I uncharacteristically swiped her hand away, insisting that I would get it.

"All right then," she uttered in a perplexed, sarcastic tone. If only she knew why I was acting strange, it would all make sense.

The loose rocks leading to the top of the hill were hard going in a wheelchair, but as ever TJ was there pushing from behind without hesitation as we slowly ground our way up the last 100 metres or so. It was in moments like this, when we were out in the wilderness as a couple in places that not many wheelchairs had dared to tread, that I reflected on how my heart had been broken by someone who couldn't see a future in which adventure would still be a possibility. That all seemed and felt like an eternity ago, aided by the fact I'd found someone who was equally determined to share in moments of adapted adventure, even if that involved some pushing on her part to make it possible!

It was what was hidden in the zip pocket behind me that was making me feel so nervous. Covertly disguised within a packet of Haribo was a ring box and within that, a Haribo ring had been placed just like a real engagement ring. But this was the real deal. Once we reached the top of the hill, I would unveil the surprise pack of sweets and TJ's hand would dive in before feeling the unexpected. At which point, I'd ask for her hand in marriage. The idea was that, once she'd said yes, we would go to the Jewellery Quarter in Birmingham to design the ring she wanted. It sounded like a good plan to me, but now that I was a matter of seconds away from asking the question, I worried I'd made the wrong decision and that she'd expect and deserve a real ring.

Murphy scampered a few metres ahead of us to the top of the hill. His long black and white fur ruffled in the light wind. Joining him at the summit and using the fact that TJ had just helped push me up the slope for the last 100 metres as cover, I asked her to take a seat on my lap. Once she'd sat down, I teased, "I've got a surprise for you," as I unzipped the pocket behind my wheelchair and proudly produced the packet of Haribo. Her eyes visibly lit up at the sight of an unexpected reward for her efforts.

"Ooh sweets!" she said happily, as her hand delved eagerly

into the bag. She immediately paused as her fingers touched the very non-Haribo-shaped dimensions of the box. Her eyes glanced up at mine. "What? What's this?" she exclaimed removing it from the bag.

I could hear the hope in her voice. Panicking that she might be expecting a diamond ring, I pre-emptively said, "It's not what you think it is."

TJ flicked open the box to reveal the Haribo ring inside. Looking up at me, she asked, "Is this a joke?"

I smiled, and simply asked, "Will you marry me?" A broad smile started to appear across her face and her eyes began to shine.

"You know I will!" she answered, throwing her arms around me.

The relief I felt on hearing her answer was unmistakable and the release of nervous tension brought an immediate return to my normal self, albeit an even more elated version! Sitting on top of one of our favourite hills, with the sprawling forested valley leading down to the lake below, we paused to take a quick selfie of TJ proudly displaying her new gummy ring before continuing the second half of our walk. "You've got to keep that on at least for the rest of the walk," I joked. Ten minutes later, and with another six or so kilometres left to go, the heavens opened. TJ's new ring quickly became sticky. To her credit, she refused to take it off even as the rain continued to fall. As far as I was concerned, the gamble had paid off – she'd said yes and we'd had a laugh in the process. With two weeks to go until the start of the Kayak 4 Heroes expedition, I'd be setting off from Land's End engaged.

21

FACING FEAR

The vast Atlantic Ocean surged before me. My eyes were fixated on its large, rolling waves breaking powerfully against the menacing rocks beneath our position. Even from our current vantage point, sitting atop one of Land's End's 300ft vertical granite rockfaces, the unbridled power these sea conditions presented was an intimidating sight. For the first time, I realised how incredibly vulnerable we would be in our small two-man sea kayaks, surrounded by such immense forces of nature. This time tomorrow, we would be somewhere out there, pitting our bodies and minds against anything and everything the sea could throw at us. I glanced at Luke standing to my left, his facial expression portraying the inner emotions all five of us were experiencing – anxiety, nervousness, self-doubt and fear. Luke summarised his feelings in a classically military turn of phrase: "That's absolutely gopping." There was no doubting the enormity of the challenge ahead of us.

It was impossible to sleep that night. With less than 12 hours to go before we embarked on the most ambitious kayaking challenge the UK had seen, I felt a certain level of responsibility on my shoulders for having led the team to this point. If anything was to go wrong in the next month, or if the ever-present risk of serious injury (or worse) was to occur, it would potentially be because of a decision I'd made. I battled constantly with the feeling of imposter syndrome as the one heading up this expedition. Yet, at the same time, I desperately wanted to lead by example, to exemplify our team's ethos of determination, perseverance, resilience and the "adapt and overcome" mindset. The next month would test the depths of my character in a very different that my life thus far had.

Penzance Harbour, bathed in the warm, orange glow of the rising sun, was a hive of activity. I readied my kit for the pivotal day ahead, checking and then double-checking that we had all the vital safety equipment our lives would depend on – Emergency Position-Indicating Radio Beacons (EPIRBs) and Very High-Frequency Radios (VHFs). Our support RIB waited for us down the slipway on the jetty. Chris had been busy putting his welding skills to use and had crafted a frame on each side of the RIB that would allow us to transport our kayaks safely across the open sea. There was a palpable sense of excitement amongst the team. Liz leant over and gave me a massive bear hug. "It's finally time to start the exped!" she exclaimed enthusiastically. Liz would be leading the efforts of the land-based support team, made up of Bob, Eddie and Kate, our team physio. With food, water, paddles and kayaks loaded, it was time to make the 15-kilometre journey to the start position, west of Land's End, at the infamous Longships Lighthouse.

As we drove away from Penzance Harbour to the distant shouts of encouragement from the support crew, the sea shimmered peacefully, beckoning us forth. There was close to no wind as we began our course around the rugged coastline of southwest Cornwall. Chris looked at me from behind the wheel, "Looking good so far. Let's hope it stays this way."

The forecast for the day was relatively good, with light winds predicted for the next 12 hours. More importantly, we had carefully timed our departure from Penzance according to the tides. Indeed, it would be tidal forces that would dictate much of our movement for the duration of the expedition. If we failed to account for the impact of the tide, which changes direction every six hours, we could face potentially life-threatening consequences. At the least severe end of the spectrum, we would still waste precious energy paddling against the flow. It was our aim to arrive off the coast of Land's End for what is known as "slack water", when the tide is at its weakest. Yet, as we rounded the headland at Porthgwarra, we saw that the waves had begun to build.

A swell was rolling in from the Atlantic. The headland around Land's End is encircled by rocks upon which countless ships have been lost; the surge of the swell was disordered as it rolled in, only to be beaten back into the sea in confusing patterns by the towering cliffs. Save for the roaring of the RIB's two engines and the splash of waves ricocheting off the boat's bow, silence had descended. Each of us sat in quiet contemplation, dwarfed by the visceral enormity of the challenge ahead of us. The erratic motion of the boat pitching in the swell proved too much for some of the team, with Luke suffering the worst effects as he repeatedly threw up over the side before reaching desperately for what unexpectedly became known as "the poo bucket".

"I've purged all the negativity," Luke joked as the team burst into fits of laughter. Inadvertently, he had helped to dispel the nervous tension onboard in the most selfless way possible.

We were approaching the Longships Lighthouse, a nineteenth-century tower rising from the sea more than a mile off the coast of Land's End. It was our intention to put the first paddling pair into the water a further two kilometres west of the tower. Jim stood next to Chris in the co-pilot chair scanning the horizon and assessing the conditions. Looking to him for his honest assessment, he confirmed, "Around here, this is as good as it's going to get." It was time to get our expedition underway! Ben and Jonny made the final tweaks to their kit, turned on their EPIRBs and VHF radios, and then drifted forward away from the RIB. It was as close as we would get to slack water on this exposed section of coastline, and we'd timed it perfectly. I sat aboard the rib, experiencing a uniquely conflicting range of emotions – overwhelming pride and excitement, yet at the same time, all-consuming self-doubt and fear. Watching Ben and Jonny battle the disorienting rise and fall of the swell, and as waves crashed against the rocky outcrop of the lighthouse on our right, I wanted nothing more than to start my first leg and calm my nerves – to prove to myself that I could do this.

Ben and Jonny performed valiantly on their maiden outing, covering close to seven kilometres in 45 minutes. They were in a buoyant mood as they clambered back aboard the RIB, the team of Ellie and Alex from Wanderlust Action Films capturing every moment of these first, ground-breaking moments. We dropped the second kayak into the water for Carl and Luke to start the next leg. Soon their Epic kayak was racing through the water, ascending the face of the rolling waves before crashing down on the other side. Like the duo before, Carl and Luke looked calm and in control. The tide was now building in our favour and helping to accelerate their kayak at an ever-increasing rate. As we began to approach the forbidding Cape Cornwall, and as I eagerly readied myself for my first stretch of open ocean, I knew that the only person I could paddle with in these conditions would be Jim. I had increasingly come to rely on his support, particularly as I found myself at the literal edge of what was possible for someone paralysed from the chest down. There would come a point in the expedition where I would feel able to step out from Jim's guidance and protection, but for now I was dependent upon his support.

Chris revved the RIB's engines as we moved ahead of Carl and Luke by a couple of hundred metres. It was time for me to put 12 months of determination, hard work and training to the test. As Ben and Jonny lowered the next kayak into the water, I shuffled on my bum across to the side of the RIB, before lowering myself into the rear seat of the kayak and tightening the straps of my adapted backrest. Ellie excitedly pointed her camera in my direction. I did my best to fake a confident smile. The tidal forces were now at their strongest, and there was a huge volume of water pushing eastward around Cape Cornwall. Jim looked over his shoulder, "Right then, Daz, let's get this show on the road," he said, using his paddle to push away from the RIB.

I could instantly feel the disorienting, disordered motion of the sea beneath us. My only means of remaining stable was to keep my paddle in a low-braced position as I tried to counteract the confusing wave patterns. After a few seconds, I gingerly took my first stroke only to quickly lose my balance. I tried again, somehow managing to string three strokes together before bracing again. Jim could feel my tension even from the front of the kayak.

"Don't try to fight the waves, just try and relax into it," he said reassuringly over his left shoulder.

"Will do!" I responded.

It felt like I was back in the swimming pool the day after

my discharge from hospital, struggling to understand how I could use my upper body to stop from capsizing. Four and a half years later, and I was still trying to solve the same problem but this time on a more adventurous and grander scale. The thought made me smile, if only for a moment. The minutes ticked by slowly as Jim and I made doggedly slow progress along the coast. I was battling with rising levels of self-doubt. *Why am I struggling so much? Why don't I look as calm and confident as the rest of the guys?* My fragile ego failed to reassert its control over the negative thought patterns. Distracted from the task at hand, I inadvertently left my paddle in the sea for a moment too long as a fresh wave rolled in and soon found myself being pulled uncontrollably by the weight of the water toward the waiting embrace of the cold Atlantic Ocean. Instinctively, I took one last sharp breath in the milliseconds before becoming submerged. This wasn't how I'd intended my expedition to start. Floating back to the surface I could see my paddle drifting away from our upturned kayak.

"Well, I wasn't expecting to get wet that soon!" Jim joked.

"Sorry Jim, I just lost it for a moment there," I responded, full of embarrassment.

Chris's voice came over the VHF radio, "Coming up on your left Daz," he transmitted. The RIB was soon approaching our position, floating five kilometres offshore. "Let's get you back on the boat," Chris shouted as he brought the RIB in close to our position. Looking at our upturned kayak, and then across at Jim, I knew that this was already a pivotal moment for me in the expedition. In this moment of adversity, staring failure firmly in the face, would I relent? The answer was simple.

"Jim, we're going to remount back into the kayak from the water," I declared confidently.

"You don't want to get back into the support boat first?" he responded quizzically.

"No. Let's do this," I responded as I flipped the boat back around.

We were about to attempt something we'd never practised in sea conditions. I reached up and over the cockpit, holding tight to the metal handle on the opposite side. Jim helped to steady the kayak as I heaved with all my might to get my body onto the seat. I could hear the shouts of encouragement from Ben, Carl, Jonny and Luke aboard the RIB. Somehow, I managed to squirm my body back into a seated position, ready for Jim to do the same. But, as he heaved himself up, we quickly lost our balance and capsized in the opposite direction. After three exhausting failed attempts, Chris threw out a safety line for us to get back to the RIB. It was a blow to my pride that we couldn't remount and carry on straight away, but as the demons of self-doubt circled in my mind, the capsize made me ever more determined to prove to myself that I could overcome this hurdle and all those that would follow. It was no different to being back on the ledge at World's End as life hung in the balance, only to make the boldest promise of a lifetime – to never give up!

22

FINDING FAITH

By the end of our first full day at sea, we had covered 55 kilometres and finished just south of the popular holiday destination of Newquay. My battle with self-doubt continued, but I had rallied and made it to the end of day one with just a single capsize to my name. There was such a fine margin of error between success and failure, between staying dry or getting wet. I had the humility to accept that I was on the steepest learning curve of all the team, and I held no delusions of grandeur that leading the team somehow made me the most competent paddler – far from it. If anything, I wanted to lead by example, even if that meant through struggle and strife, and a refusal to give up. As we headed into the picturesque harbour of Newquay aboard the RIB, I confided in Carl that I'd felt like the weak link that day. Carl's response spoke volumes about the camaraderie within our team: "There's no such thing as a weak link," he affirmed reassuringly.

After our eventful day on the water, and as everyone's levels of adrenaline started to subside, we had no issue with falling asleep that night – if only for a few precious hours. Once again, the tide dictated our plans for the following day, which meant that we'd be leaving Newquay at 05:00. As the sun slowly rose over the horizon and an early morning mist hung majestically above the still water, we motored out through the stone harbour walls, the RIB tracking our course back to where we'd finished the previous day. Spirits were high. Day one proved that, despite our personal struggles, we could achieve our target of 50 kilometres in a single day. Keen to take advantage of the forecast for low winds over the next few hours, I said that Jim and I would get us underway for the day. Bolstered by the relative success of only falling in once yesterday and with a gentle wind blowing in our favour, I was confident about the day ahead.

It took a few minutes for my body to warm into the early-morning start, but soon my strokes began to match Jim's, my right blade cutting through the water at the same time as his, and then our left in unison. For the first time since we'd started the expedition together, I felt like I was able to help propel the boat faster through the water instead of simply focussing on trying to keep us from capsizing. I could feel the difference in speed and was even able to relax my tensed shoulders and look across at the rugged, prehistoric coastline to our right. To be here was an absolute privilege. Each moment was a gift that so easily could have not happened, for a million and one different reasons.

The RIB hung in close proximity behind us, the low hum from its twin engines an audible reassurance that, should anything go wrong, the team would be right on hand. As I slowly began to rebuild my levels of confidence and self-belief in this latest bold endeavour, I drew strength from the incredible team around me; the bonds created in the pursuit of a shared goal are incredibly powerful.

Spirits were high as we made progress up the beautiful Cornish coastline and headed for the high, rocky outcrop of Hartland Point in Devon. The team were quickly adapting to the routine of expedition life: rotating paddlers every 45 minutes, eating, living and even sleeping on a small boat packed with kit and equipment for six paddlers plus the film crew of Ellie and Alex. It was a cramped existence, but a happy one. Thankfully, there had been no need for Luke's poo bucket to emerge since the first day and it appeared that everyone had firmly found their sea legs. Chris continued to make full use of the most important aspect of his responsibility as Captain of our safety RIB, which frequently resulted in Jonny questionably gyrating to the club anthem *Purple Hat* by Sofi Tukker pumping from the RIB's speakers. For those of us who were forced to bear witness, not sure whether Jonny was suffering from extreme heatstroke or had mixed the wrong powder into his isotonic drink that morning, it suddenly became apparent what the women of Kingsbridge, Devon had been subjected to since his coming of age. By the time it came for Jim and me to prepare for the final 45-minute rotation of the day before the tide started to work against us, we had covered close to 60 kilometres. As predicted, the wind had remained incredibly subdued and the water was personified by a gentle, rolling calmness. We had outperformed all our expectations, but we knew that our luck with the weather wasn't going to last indefinitely.

Once Jim and I had clocked up a further seven kilometres to finish the day, we made the short, fast journey back to Penzance Harbour aboard the RIB. We were welcomed into the harbour by a chorus of cheers from those lining the bank. Surprised by the unexpected moment of celebrity, our inner regalness awakened as we waved back courteously. Unsurprisingly, our land-based support crew were the masterminds behind this rousing reception. Bob and Liz had spoken to anyone and everyone ahead of our arrival, telling them about our epic undertaking. Yet, this turned out to be the tip of the iceberg of what had happened since we'd left Newquay bright and early that morning.

"You have no idea what you've missed!" Liz exclaimed in fits of laughter.

Bob took great pride in filling in the gaps: "The van engine blew up, the boat trailer started falling apart and we've been back and forth to the mechanics like headless chickens! I thought you guys were meant to have the hard job, not us!"

It was a timely reminder that the fate of the expedition didn't entirely depend on what we achieved on the water because without a functioning support crew on land, we'd fall apart at the seams.

My briefing to the team later that night was somewhat less optimistic for the days ahead. A weather front was moving in, bringing with it higher winds at a crucial stage in our expedition – the exposed crossing from the prominent headland of Hartland Point across to the infamous Morte Point (*morte* meaning death in French). Wind speeds of up to 25 kilometres per hour were predicted by midday, which was at the very limit of the conditions we were capable of handling. Regardless, we would head out early in the RIB to assess conditions and make an informed judgement call as to the level of acceptable risk. Leaving from the concrete slipway in Appledore in North Devon the next morning, we headed out of the sheltered bay for Hartland Point. Protected from the winds by the coastline to our left, the RIB sped effortlessly across the gentle waves as both of its engines whirred in unison. All looked manageable thus far. But, as we began to chart a course around the headland and back toward yesterday's finish point, waves began to build in both frequency and size. The RIB began to slam down onto the water as the waves broke underneath. Sitting in the co-pilot chair next to Chris, my grip on the metal handrail in front of me tightened. The boat was taking some significant punishment. Before it was too late, Jim interjected. "The prediction is that the wind is going to rise and the waves are going to get steeper. The waves will double in size." The team agreed, it was time to turn around and head for safe harbour.

The sea churned white and black around us. The hull of the RIB slammed mercilessly against the cresting waves. As Jim predicted, the waves grew steeper than before, angrier than before. The twin engines roared out of sync as the boat pitched slightly one way and then the other. I couldn't believe how quickly conditions had changed; just 30 minutes ago we were considering launching the first kayak into the water, now just half an hour later, even the RIB was struggling to make significant headway without taking a battering. Suddenly, the kayak suspended above the port side of the RIB dropped into the water, the frame upon which it had sat broken under the force of the last wave. The collapsed V-shaped frame bobbed in the sea behind us. Luckily, Ben and Luke had been well placed to stop the kayak from being damaged. The tension was palpable. Jim stood close behind me, his hand firm on top of my buoyancy aid. He hadn't said anything, but I knew that he was readying himself to help me in the event of the RIB capsizing. Thankfully, we made it back around the headland and retreated to the safety of the Appledore estuary. High winds would prevent us from attempting the next stage of our expedition until the day after tomorrow. Until then, all we could do was plan, rest and recover.

Our fortunes turned on what would be the fifth day of our expedition. With subdued winds forecast for the duration of the morning, we picked up from where we left off two days earlier, five kilometres offshore southwest of Bude. We were in a race against the clock to get past the stretch of treacherous water around Hartland Point. The first two hours of the day would be against a slowing tide, giving us the best chance of avoiding any greater risk by the time we arrived at infamous Morte Point. Just five days into our challenge, the team was a slick, well-oiled machine. Working to our 45-minute clock, the team rallied selflessly around whomever was next out on the water, ensuring that no initiative or time was lost as we progressed up the coastline. Carl and Luke raced ahead of the RIB as they kayaked past the domineering, vertical rockface of Hartland Point, its white lighthouse perched at the very edge of the rock-strewn headland. The tidal flow against them was minimal, and with fully rested bodies, they effortlessly cut through the water together. Yet, the further we pushed past Hartland, the easier it became to see the ruthless turmoil that Morte Point was about to present. The headland was dominated by menacing black rocks, with a short gap through which we had to pass between jagged cliffs and a dangerous cluster of rocks emerging from the sea. Our horizon was now full of the chaotic disorder of waves breaking against cliffs, which in turn, smashed against the island of rocks. It looked as if the sea was angry to be disturbed.

Being the Expedition Leader, I wanted to tackle the intimidating stretch before us with Jim. Yet, the realist in me knew that I needed to have the humility to accept that, of everyone in the team, I represented the greatest risk of failure or serious injury – not just to myself, but to all the team if they became embroiled in a rescue mission in the jaws of "death point". It had earnt its reputation for a reason.

"While I want to sit in that rear seat and risk that I'll make it through, I know that it's not what is best for the team," I said to everyone sitting aboard the RIB as we plotted our strategy for the pivotal next leg.

One of Jim's main motives for joining as part of the expedition team was to ensure that we made it through the most dangerous moments of our route unscathed, and this was perhaps the single greatest moment of danger.

"I'm happy to sit in the front seat and keep the kayak on the best line possible," he said from the rear of the RIB.

"I'll go through with him," Ben added selflessly. It was decided.

Even though I wouldn't be paddling the next leg, my stomach turned over with nerves. Watching Jim and Ben paddle toward the horizon, and as the RIB hovered protectively behind the pair, the deafening sound of waves breaking against rock filled the air. Mercilessly battering the tiny, exposed kayak the waves came from what seemed like all directions. Those of us aboard the RIB readied the safety throw lines just in case we needed to react quickly.

"I'm not comfortable. This is too bloody dangerous," Chris remarked.

Ben was doing his best to stay stable, keeping his paddle low and braced against the water as it lashed powerfully against his blade. Jim drove the kayak forward, all his years of experience paddling across the world coming into sharp focus. After what felt like an eternity, thankfully the pair emerged through the worst and into clearer waters beyond the headland. Chris pulled the RIB in close to their kayak, allowing them to lean on its soft, rubber side before getting off the water. Ben and Jim puffed out their cheeks tellingly, laughing as they did so. There was a huge release of tension both off and on the boat. The words "gnarly", "epic" and "gopping" were uttered more than once. We'd overcome a huge test passing through the gates of hell at Morte Point, and most importantly we'd come through unscathed.

Like the mountains, the sea can be a foreboding, menacing place. Yet, at the same time, it also presents an opportunity for self-discovery I'd once thought only existed high on a windswept peak. Later that day, as I paddled toward Combe Martin and the entrance to the vast Bristol Channel, a series of waves rolled in from the rear. As they accelerated behind us, the power of the water began to propel the kayak forward. "Paddle, Paddle, Paddle!" roared Jim from the front seat. I dug my blades deep into the water, feeling the connection with each stroke and using the force of the water to push against it. The speedometer clipped to my footwell started to tick frantically upward: 15 kilometres per hour, 17 kilometres per hour, 20 kilometres per hour. Soon, we were surging on top of a wave at 24 kilometres per hour. The raw sense of adrenaline and speed was unrivalled as our small kayak powered forward. I felt poised, stable and very much the master of my own destiny as we rode wave after wave, using Mother Nature to speed us toward our goal. From a sense of shattered self-confidence on day one of the expedition, I had found a physical and mental resolve beyond what I'd thought possible just days earlier.

Before us now stood the second-largest tidal range in the world, the Bristol Channel. Buoyed by the success with which we'd navigated the "shipwreck coast" of Cornwall and North Devon, we set out across the murky, brown waters of the Bristol Channel. The sheer volume of water flooding in and out of the Channel every six hours would be both an asset and a hindrance. At its best, strong tidal forces pushed us further east and toward the towering Prince of Wales bridge separating England and Wales at the mouth of the River Severn. With these massive lunar forces behind us, we made quick progress toward the bridge, a place that marked the end of the first 350 kilometres of our expedition. At its worst, the tide combined with rising wind speeds to make conditions considerably tougher. However, just seven days since setting off from the tip of the Atlantic Ocean at Land's End, I paddled under the sprawling mass of the Prince of Wales Bridge. Small whirlpools dragged and corkscrewed beneath the kayak, but I felt calm and confident. So many people had told me that I'd never get to experience or see this moment, that we would have failed long before reaching the end of the Bristol Channel, and that I would be the weak link dragging the team back. They were wrong. They were very wrong.

23

NERVOUS MOMENTS

Reaching the end of the first phase of our expedition, we had achieved way beyond our modest expectations. Frustratingly for Liz, this had meant that for every day we managed to unexpectedly cover more distance than planned (which was every day thus far), she would spend the afternoon frantically trying to rebook accommodation for that evening. True to form, she took it all in her stride, powered by nothing more than Diet Coke and unrelenting enthusiasm. But before we could start the second phase of the expedition, which would see us paddle over 250 kilometres inland to Liverpool and the Irish Sea, it was only right that we signed off on an incredibly successful first week with a well-deserved beer and BBQ. It was also an opportunity to say thank you and farewell to Bob and Eddie, who had kept their spirits high even when everything around them seemed to be blowing up or falling apart!

I was excited to start the next leg of our expedition, not only because our movements would no longer be subject to winds and tides, but because it would give me the opportunity to build confidence paddling with the rest of the team. Luke and I had actively avoided paddling together since capsizing in the middle of Lake Windermere in April. It made sense to shake off memories of Windermere's cold embrace and share a boat together again.

"This already feels so different to the last time we paddled together, mate," Luke said over his shoulder as we headed over refreshingly flat water toward Gloucester.

"Is that because we're currently not upside down?" I joked in response.

"There's still time!" Luke replied, laughing.

In the days that followed, as we slowly worked our way along the pristine banks of the River Severn, it became apparent that the peace and tranquillity of our new surroundings provided a rare opportunity to connect at a deeper level and on a one-to-one basis with the team. Ben and I were paddling through the pristine wilderness toward Worcester when he confided that becoming part of the Kayak 4 Heroes team had helped save him from his battles with depression and mental health. It was a humbling reminder that the impact of this expedition extended far beyond the physical act of kayaking those 1,400 kilometres.

In a feat of superhuman endurance, it took us just three days to kayak 250 kilometres from the end of the Bristol Channel to the edge of the industrial hub of Ellesmere Port, adjacent to Liverpool and the Mersey. In the past 24 hours alone, we'd covered over 100 kilometres and portaged (carried) our kayaks around more than 50 canal locks and bridges. Unsurprisingly, we were all starting to feel the physical effects of such rapid progress. My shoulders were tight and my muscles sore after ten days of taxing physical exertion, but thankfully my historically dodgy shoulder was holding up well against the physicality of expedition life. Already four days ahead of schedule, we decided to take this opportunity to have a well-deserved rest in Liverpool before regrouping with the RIB once more on the banks of the Mersey 24 hours later. Ahead of us awaited the longest and toughest part of our route, which would see us paddle across the Irish Sea and into the rugged beauty of southwest Scotland. As we basked in the warm afternoon sun outside a pub on the Royal Albert Dock, little did we know what truly lay ahead. We would be lucky to emerge unscathed.

A low, grey mist hung over Liverpool the next morning. Heading into the next big sea leg of our expedition, I was full of confidence that I would be able to start kayaking with more of the team out at sea. I'd already overcome what I believed would be the most pivotal moments of this challenge and I'd continued to build levels of self-belief with each day that passed. The Mersey was already a hub of activity by the time we dropped the first pair – Jonny and Jim – onto the water. As they paddled along the historic dockyard, with the iconic backdrop of Victoria Tower soaring overhead, the pair passed by a vast cruise ship moored against the jetty. From our vantage point aboard the RIB, I suddenly came to appreciate the extent to which our small, white Epic kayaks would be dwarfed by some of the traffic crossing from the northwest of England to Ireland and Scotland – we would be very much in their territory from now on.

The low roar of the RIB's twin engines permeated the atmosphere and we were soon racing past Jonny and Jim. Carl and I readied our kayak and safety equipment in anticipation of beginning our first leg at the mouth of the Mersey. "Remember, just take your time to relax into it and try not to fight against the waves," Carl said in his calm, reassuring manner. Since we had first announced our bold plan to kayak from Land's End to John O' Groats a little over twelve months ago, I'd paddled with Carl more than anyone else in the team and had come to rely on his calming presence in some of our more nerve-testing moments.

While the mist had yet to lift, the sea was fortuitously calm and bobbed gently beneath us as we headed away from the RIB and along the sandy shore to our right. I felt calm, composed and, most importantly, stable. Kilometres passed underneath our boat with ease as we headed toward the distant landmark of Blackpool Tower sitting on the horizon. On my next rotation, I paddled with Ben beyond Blackpool and towards the treacherous Morecambe Bay, made infamous by the 2004 disaster in which 23 individuals drowned. We took the opportunity to reflect on our journey to date and spoke in depth about the challenges of mental health: how hard it can be to ask for help and how difficult it is to be vulnerable and open about our internal struggles. One thing was for sure, we were both wealthier emotionally for having the Kayak 4 Heroes expedition and family in our lives.

Finishing our day just south of Morecambe Bay and ready to tackle the crossing tomorrow, I felt a huge sense of achievement for what I'd just achieved. I'd stepped out from beneath Jim's wing, where he had helped keep me safe as I battled to adjust and improve and I was now confident and capable enough to start paddling with the others as well. We were greeted with a hero's welcome as we de-bussed from the RIB at the small fishing village of Knott-End-on-Sea. Liz had been hard at work once more and before we knew it, we had been invited to join the lovely ladies of Knott-End-on-Sea Golf Club at their exclusive (or at least it was until we turned up) Ladies Day, which now featured a team of bearded men eagerly demolishing sandwiches, chips, cakes – or anything that came to our table – as we relaxed in the warm afternoon sun. It was a lovely way to end a first successful day back out at sea, and we left later that afternoon with full bellies and even fuller hearts.

Over the course of the next few days, we continued our surging progress along the Cumbrian coastline. Morecambe Bay had played kindly as we made the 30-kilometre crossing at low tide across its vast bay and I continued to build on the belief that the limits I'd placed on myself were so inaccurate; I was capable of so much more than I'd ever given myself credit for. As I paddled through the mountainous landscape of the Lake District, and as another successful day ended – and with it a further 70 kilometres under our belts – there was a decision to make for the next day that would have potentially expedition-altering consequences. And it needed to be one that the whole team were comfortable with.

The Solway Firth forms part of the border between England and Scotland, between Cumbria and Dumfries and Galloway. The original route-plan I had formulated from my kitchen table some twelve months ago suggested that we hug the coastline of the Solway Firth for the next three days until we would reach the southerly Scottish seaport of the Isle of Whithorn. If we were bold, however, we could save two days by heading directly across the Irish Sea from Ravenglass, Cumbria to the Isle of Whithorn. But this 70-kilometre crossing would be an epic undertaking that could leave us drastically exposed and more than 30 kilometres from the nearest safe harbour should the worst happen. The forecast for the next day looked good, with low winds and a manageable wave height predicted for the eight to ten hours it might take us to reach the distant Isle of Whithorn. In Whitehaven later that evening, eating dinner as a team, we decided to be bold.

I stared across the expanse of water ahead of us. There was no sight of land on the horizon. A stillness hung over the water, and the absence of wind or wave gave the sea a rare sense of calm as the early-morning sun struggled to break through the clouds overhead. Ben and I powered forward, keen to make the most of the ideal conditions. The further we got from shore, the less significant our small two-person kayak seemed, dwarfed as it was by the enormous volume of water around us. With no reference point on the horizon for us to head toward, the RIB charted a course for us to follow. For the remainder of our day, we would be dependent on the RIB for navigating across to the Isle of Whithorn. The stubborn cloud cover grew angrier and darker the further we delved into the crossing. Time seemed to pass more slowly now that we were deprived of physical land references or objects to distract us from the endless hours of paddling. Midway through our voyage across the Irish Sea, roughly four hours after setting off from the coast of Cumbria, we became increasingly concerned by the deteriorating weather now surrounding us.

“In the last half an hour visibility has dropped from what I’d call ‘good’ to a matter of two hundred metres in all directions,” Jim said from the front seat of our kayak. Moving my paddle through the slate-grey water, I glanced around to see nothing but a wall of mist a couple of hundred metres from our position. The rise and fall of the RIB on the ever-rising waves ahead had become noticeably less visible than when Jim and I had started our rotation together.

“So, what do we do if things continue to deteriorate?” I asked in response, an inflexion of concern in my voice.

“We think of an exit strategy and run for shore on the RIB,” Jim replied, all his years of experience mitigating risk at sea and on expeditions like this coming to the fore.

The reality was, even though the RIB could continue to navigate in indefinitely hostile conditions with no visibility thanks to its GPS unit, there would be no way of knowing whether a car or passenger ferry was bearing down on our position, and there would be no way to manoeuvre our boats out of the way in time to avoid catastrophe.

Climbing aboard the RIB at the end of our rotation, and with Carl and Luke now manning the next leg, Jim shared his thoughts with Chris about the need for an exit strategy should conditions continue to worsen. The three of us crowded around the small GPS plotter unit as the RIB continued its direct line to the Scottish mainland hidden some 35 kilometres away in the mist ahead of us. Technically, we were as close to the Isle of Man as we were to Scotland or England, but wherever our Plan B would be, we'd need to be able to resupply with Liz and the vehicles. No more than a few minutes of deliberation had passed between the three of us before Ben called urgently from his position at the rear of the RIB. "Guys, we've lost sight of Carl and Luke."

Hearing Ben's words filled my heart with dread and I quickly turned round from the co-pilot seat. I paused unintentionally for a moment in stunned silence as I stared at the impenetrable sheet of white mist that now hung just 50 metres from the rear of our boat. As Ben had identified, there was no sight of the small two-man team trailing behind the RIB… at least we hoped it was still behind us. I instinctively grabbed at the VHF radio clipped to the front of my buoyancy aid. "Carl, Luke, this is Darren. Can you confirm that you have a visual on the RIB?" We waited nervously for their reply as Chris slowed the RIB's twin engines to idling and the rest of us impatiently eyed the wall of white separating us from our teammates. Seconds passed at an excruciatingly slow rate. No reply came. I thumbed at the receiver button on my radio again, sending the same hopeful message for the second time. No response. "Carl, Luke. Radio check. Over," I repeated in the vague hope that they could still hear us. A pang of guilt washed over me. What if this moment of worry escalated to something more serious? Could I forgive myself for dragging Carl and Luke across the Irish Sea with me to chase a wide-eyed dream of kayaking from Land's End to John O' Groats?

Five minutes had now passed since my first message over the VHF. Each minute stretched like an eternity. Chris revved the RIB's engines as he spun the boat around in the water ready to re-trace our previous course. Six pairs of eyes impatiently scanned the horizon, desperate to glimpse a flash of the orange buoyancy aids or white paint of the kayak. Alas, all that we could see was mist. Silence blanketed the RIB, save for the low rumble of its engines. With every metre we backtracked, and with no sign of Carl and Luke, there was a mounting sense of urgency and desperation. The stark reality was that right now Carl and Luke could be capsized in deteriorating conditions in the middle of the Irish Sea and even if they were still upright, with no visual aid to navigate by they could be headed toward Northern Ireland over 100 kilometres away. Jim indicated to Chris that we should head back to our previous position before we considered our escalation process. I began to fear the worst, my brain punishing me with different versions of a worst-case scenario. Suddenly, Jonny's voice penetrated the silence. "I can see them! They're at our nine o-clock!" Our heads spun in unison as our spirits lifted in hope. Through the dense mist and haze, there was a flash of orange against the grey. It was them! We shouted out across the water and I jumped back on the radio for good measure. Seconds later, the kayak turned towards our position and headed toward the RIB. There was an immediate release of tension aboard, and I'd never been so pleased to see my teammates.

The drama of the Irish Sea signalled the beginning of what

would become a challenging section of the expedition for many of the team. Although we successfully made the crossing in eight hours, and had saved two days paddling as predicted, we'd had a harsh lesson in playing with forces far bigger than ourselves. Until the Irish Sea, we'd largely benefitted from mild to moderate conditions, all within the realms of capability for our RIB floating support island. Chris had proved an astute and intelligent captain and had handled his boat with calm professionalism in moments of adversity. Yet, as we set off across the Clyde Sea from the port town of Stranraer towards the rugged shoreline of the Isle of Arran, Chris was about to face his toughest challenge yet.

Leaving the dockyard in Stranraer, Jonny and I powered forward along the length of Loch Ryan, heading for the open sea. Our spirits were high, and we made light of the trials and tribulations of recent days with a dark sense of humour that the military community tends to thrive on. On the horizon, we could see the lone volcanic island of Ailsa Craig protruding from the sea. The closer we journeyed to the mouth of the Loch, I could see that the currents were beginning to converge, accentuated by a slowly rising wind that cut across our bow. In this environment, conditions had the potential to change quickly. An hour later, it was now Jim and Jonny battling across increasingly hostile waves. From my position next to Chris, we quickly loaded up an up-to-date weather forecast. Frustratingly, winds were forecast to continue rising and the tide would now be flowing directly against the prevailing winds – this meant bigger, sharper waves. I signalled across to Jim as their kayak slid off the back of the previous wave. It was time to cut our losses for the day and head back to a safe harbour while we still could.

With everyone back aboard the RIB and the kayaks strapped

down, Chris headed north toward the port of Campbelltown some 30 kilometres from our current position. Within a matter of minutes, the whole surface of the sea had become a dizzy whirl of rushing, bounding, crashing rage. Chris fought to keep the RIB from being broadsided by the steep waves now cascading in our direction. The force of the water slamming against the hull sent a sharp wave of vibration through all of us. My hand gripped the metal bar in front of me. We were a little boat at the mercy of the sea, entirely dependent on Chris's skills if we were to emerge unscathed. A few minutes later, having not uttered a word since our situation worsened, Chris looked at me with concern and said, "It's 50/50 whether we're going to make this out in one piece. I just want to be real with you." I wasn't sure how to respond, or whether he expected me to or not, but as the next wave slammed against the hull tipping the boat momentarily off balance, I looked anxiously at the cluttered confines of the cockpit around me. Would I be able to extricate myself from my current position if the RIB flipped upside down? As if he knew what was going through my mind, Chris said, "Don't worry, if anything happens and you get stuck, I'm not leaving you behind."

There was such little margin for error; one wrong decision and Chris could have flipped the RIB and our once safe floating island would have been history, our expedition and potentially our lives along with it. Thankfully, a little over a heart-wrenching hour later, we made it through the worst and into the calmer waters off the coast of Campbeltown. I looked at Chris and simply said, "I bloody love you." Although we had arrived battered and bruised, and with our egos once more in check, it did present us with an opportunity for some light entertainment. It had become apparent that my wheelchair was still more than six hours from Campbeltown. Always up for a challenge, Luke and Jonny scanned the dockyard around us, then leapt from the RIB and momentarily disappeared down the jetty. They returned triumphantly moments later with what appeared to be the solution to my current mobility problems – a trolley from B&Q. With six hours to wait until our support crew arrived, I sat proudly on my trolley and was treated to a tour of the town before entering a pub to the bemused smiles of the locals as we explained who the hell we were and why one of us was riding a gardening trolley. The most testing moment of our expedition had led, in turn, to one of the silliest. Thank God for B&Q.

24

THE SUMMIT

The bow of my kayak surged forward, carving through the tranquillity of the water ahead of us. I breathed the crisp, fresh mountain air and felt the hairs on my arms stand to attention in the early morning chill. As we slowly began to weave our way through a series of interlinking lochs and island passageways leading to Fort William, a large pod of bottle-nose Dolphins frolicked and leapt gleefully behind us. I was surrounded by the very best of Scotland's rugged, wild beauty and I couldn't have been happier. A broad, unapologetic smile beamed from my face with each stroke of my paddle through the water. Five years had passed since I'd been admitted to the ICU at Stoke Hospital and in those dark, intimidating moments, the thought had occurred to me that my life might never be the same again. And yet, here I was, only a few years later, challenging myself once more, risking failure once more, and chasing a dream once more. In all the ways that mattered most, my life hadn't changed at all.

We passed along the jagged peaks of the Isle of Mull's eastern shore, before paddling through the bustling port of Oban, adorned with its multi-coloured harbour frontage reminiscent of Denmark or Sweden. A variety of boat traffic buzzed around us, everything from authentic, small fishing boats to gigantic car ferries heading to the Inner and Outer Hebrides. We were now no more than 50 kilometres from Fort William, which served as the launching point for the final phase of our expedition that would see us paddle across the length of the world-famous Caledonian Canal, including the windswept shores of Loch Ness, before setting sail to John O' Groats on the last of Great Britain's wild seas – the North Sea.

The Kayak 4 Heroes team was 21 days and over 1,200 kilometres into its unproven, world-first expedition. Each day we put our bodies on the line, grafting selflessly and willingly for the men beside us. From day one, humour had been at the heart of our morale. In the moments that mattered most, we had managed to find cheerfulness in adversity and had joked and jested relentlessly with each other in both our highest and lowest moments. When my confidence had been at rock bottom earlier in our challenge, Jonny sat next to me and gave me a genuine, supportive hug before injecting his trademark sense of humour: "I draw the line at hugs, mate. I don't kiss blokes, even if it'll make them feel better."

Falling short of Fort William that afternoon, cut off by the racing tidal waters of the Corran Narrows, we regrouped as a team in yet another nondescript car park to formulate a plan for the following day. Day 22 would be a mammoth physical and logistical undertaking – to kayak over 110 kilometres from the Corran Narrows to Inverness and the gateway to the North Sea. We would be covering this massive distance without the dedicated support of the RIB, which we would be transported ahead of us by road to Inverness. Knowing that we could be on the water for close to 12 hours, we set off amidst the melodic dawn chorus. I'd read online about the majestic beauty of the Caledonian Canal, which connects the west and east coasts of Scotland through a series of manmade canals and expansive natural bodies of water (Loch Lochy, Loch Oich and Loch Ness). Paddling along the luscious green banks of the canal lined by tall pine trees leading from Fort William to Loch Lochy (what a great name), I remarked to Carl about how I'd learnt to kayak on a canal like this one just weeks after my discharge from the Midland Centre for Spinal Injuries. It was a poignant and beautiful moment of self-reflection. "You should be very proud of yourself, Darren," Carl said. "You've come a long way."

There are certain moments in an expedition that you will remember forever. These aren't necessarily flashes of greatest adrenaline where everything hangs in the balance or seconds of heart-pounding adversity, but they still have a deep connection at an emotional level. For me, paddling across Loch Ness with Luke was one of those such moments. From the pair who had suffered a crisis of confidence after capsizing on Lake Windermere, we had made an unfathomable improvement in our ability to kayak together.

"What the hell has happened to us?" Luke said as he laughed over his shoulder. "This is the most stable I've felt with anyone on the whole expedition!" Instead of simply battling to stay upright, we were pushing harder and faster as we raced with a newly discovered sense of confidence toward Inverness.

"Shall we just save the rest of the lads the trouble and finish the expedition off together?" I joked playfully.

Buoyed by the success of our epic day on the Caledonian Canal, we headed out later that evening to cheer on England at the delayed Euro 2020 final against Italy. Arriving at a packed pub outside Inverness, it quickly became apparent that the partisan crowd of Scottish locals would be firmly supporting the Italian side. Very much flying the flag solo for England, our small team commandeered a corner of the pub in the hope of watching history being made on the pitch that night. Unfortunately, despite our best efforts, England stayed true to form and went on to lose on penalties. Alas, it would be left to us to make history, and we were now less than 200 kilometres from our goal – the elusive John O' Groats.

"Don't kid yourselves that success is now a foregone conclusion," Jim warned, addressing the team. "The North Sea can be a wild and unforgiving place. It shouldn't be taken lightly." There was no room for complacency and the sea didn't care if we were a stone's throw from success; it was still a law unto itself. Twenty-three days into our expedition, and after the mammoth efforts of the previous days, exhaustion and fatigue had become an ever-present reality for the team. Personally, the demanding physical nature of the expedition waged a constant battle of attrition on my arms and shoulders. I was having to dig deeper into my reserves with each day that passed. Yet, as I rode the strong tidal currents out of Inverness and across the beginning of the vast Moray Firth with Ben, I found strength in knowing that, however depleted my body might be, however exacting the days that would follow, I wouldn't give up. Like many occasions before, I would rely on my determined, resilient mindset to drag me across the finish line.

The sea churned and twisted beneath me as it pulled and dragged the rear of our kayak. We were locked in a battle to maintain our direction of travel, a duel between two people and the anarchy of enormous power being thrown at us. Our position was roughly five kilometres offshore from Scotland's northeast coastline as we charted a course toward the final harbour of our expedition before John O' Groats. Jim expertly controlled the rudder to prevent us from being hit side-on and rolled over by the rising waves. Sitting at the rear, I drove my paddle powerfully through the water, pushing, pulling, and bracing with enough force to help ensure we didn't fall victim to the dominance of the sea. With each surge of nature's wild, unbridled power, I found myself revelling in the visceral rush of my body's response to the danger around us. Adrenaline was pulsing through my veins and my mind became laser focused as my sympathetic nervous system flooded my body with the concoction of chemicals we refer to as the fight or flight response. I was now able to handle conditions far more challenging than I ever thought possible at the start of the expedition. After what felt like an eternity, the intensity of the waves began to subside and we were able to reunite with the RIB without fear of colliding with each other as we attempted to dismount.

Three days after departing from Inverness, we reached the quaint fishing village of Wick. We were now a mere 35 kilometres from John O' Groats. I couldn't believe it. Over the course of the last 25 days, we had journeyed across some of the toughest and wildest waters in Europe – the Atlantic Ocean, the Bristol Channel, the Irish Sea and finally the North Sea. At times, we had been locked in epic duels with the sea, but we had also overcome internal battles and struggles with our confidence, self-belief, self-doubt, mental health, and even imposter syndrome. We'd come a long way as individuals and as a team.

Waking just before 05:00 the next morning, we pulled on our kit and prepared the RIB for the last time. However, there was one question on everyone's mind – which four members of the team would get the opportunity to paddle across the finish line into John O' Groats? "Guys, I don't think it'd be right for me to claim one of the four spots just because I'm the Expedition Leader. I don't want to rob you of that moment," I told everyone as we stood in the sharp morning air, preparing to slip our mooring on the quayside. I owed everything to my team. It had been the honour of a lifetime to lead Ben, Carl, Luke and Jonny on this truly wonderful journey, and it would be the proudest moment of my life to see them take our two tiny kayaks over the line at John O' Groats.

We basked in the sun's warm glow as we began our final voyage. A large colony of puffins perched on the towering, jagged cliffs to our left, the flawless white of their chests contrasting brightly against the earthy brown rock upon which they nested. The natural beauty of this stretch of coastline had taken us all by surprise, and we had fallen in love with this far-flung outpost of the Scottish mainland. Conditions remained incredibly calm, with a gentle rolling swell accompanying us on the final kilometres of this most epic of adventures. There was only time for one last 45-minute rotation before we reached Duncansby Head, the rocky gateway to John O' Groats. Grabbing my gear, I switched on the VHF radio strapped to my buoyancy aid for the last time and lowered myself into the kayak where a smiling Carl was waiting for me. It was a surreal mixture of emotions knowing that our expedition was ending, that we were on the cusp of achieving something historic, and that in doing so we would close the most exciting chapter of my life. I was hit by a pang of emotion, a profound realisation that regardless of the adversity we'd faced, I'd treasure these moments for the rest of my life. This team was my family.

Carl and I paddled together in beautiful harmony with the gentle rise and fall of the sea, the sunlight reflecting majestically across the glimmering surface of the water. No longer were we locked in a battle with the elements; if anything, it felt like we were being rewarded for our efforts and warmly embraced by Mother Nature. Our paddles glided effortlessly, silently, through the water in perfect unison. My body felt perfectly poised, totally balanced despite the small undulations of swell beneath me. I felt like a completely different person from the nervous, timid man who had set off from Land's End wondering if he could possibly achieve the enormous challenge ahead of him. I was more confident, more emboldened than ever before. For the first time, I allowed myself to think about life beyond the expedition – the incredible things I now felt confident I could go on to achieve in the future. Our journey had taught me that I was capable of achieving far more than I'd ever thought possible.

I took my place aboard the RIB next to Chris for the final time. Jim perched beside me on the boat's edge. Both kayaks were in the water and headed for John O' Groats, now only a couple of hundred metres away. Chris pulled the RIB alongside Ben and Jonny who danced joyfully, holding their paddles in the air, and almost capsizing in the process. Ellie sat at the bow of the RIB capturing every second of our triumphant arrival. Leaning over to Chris, I gratefully patted him on the back and said, "We couldn't have done this without you, mate. Thank you for keeping us safe." Turning to face Jim, I smiled warmly and held out my hand. "Jim, without you, I couldn't have done this. You gave me the strength to believe. For that, I will ever be grateful." We could hear the distant cheers and shouts of encouragement from the harbour wall, where a Kayak 4 Heroes flag had been unfurled by Liz. I wiped away tears of pride as I watched the team arrive at the concrete slipway marking the end of our extraordinary journey. They were ecstatic, embracing each other warmly as they waited for the RIB to arrive. The guys lifted me over the RIB's rubber side for the last time, reuniting me with my wheelchair before nearly knocking me out of it with their overly enthusiastic hugs. I felt overwhelmed by pride at what we had achieved and enormous gratitude to be surrounded by such good people.

We happily posed for pictures beneath the iconic signpost, including one fantastic image of the entire Kayak 4 Heroes family crowded happily together. One thing was for certain, without the tireless support of Liz, Kate, Neil and those who had so selflessly given their time throughout the course of the expedition, this moment wouldn't have happened. There had been so many times when the expedition faced potential ruin, whether that was the van's engine blowing up, the RIB's trailer falling to pieces, or the sheer logistical nightmare of managing a challenge of such scale, Liz and the team had taken it all in their stride, never once allowing adversity to negatively define the outcome of the expedition.

The puzzled looks from those waiting their turn to take a picture next to the signpost suggested that, on this one rare occasion, Liz hadn't managed to speak to absolutely everyone in the harbour ahead of our arrival. Heading across the car park to get changed, I was stopped by a lady and her husband who were keen to know what all the commotion was about. "Have you come far?" they asked inquisitively. Replying, "Only Cornwall," the couple visibly stopped in their tracks, trying to decide whether the beaming smile on my face was from a genuine sense of achievement, or if I was light-heartedly having them on. However, it wasn't much longer before all of John O' Groats was awash with talk of what the five weather-beaten men had just achieved – history.

I'd once dreamt of climbing the world's tallest mountain and standing on the summit of Mount Everest. Life had however taken me on a different, unexpected path. And yet, as I sat below the famous signpost at John O' Groats, I realised I had achieved far more than I ever could have on the perilous, snow-covered slopes of Everest. I hadn't just survived 26 gruelling, tough days at sea paddling across the length of Great Britain, I had overcome five years of physically and mentally exacting rehabilitation as I built a life full of purpose and passion in the aftermath of the climbing accident that left me paralysed from the chest down. I had stood to lose everything, and yet I had lost nothing. Thanks to those around me, from the incredible network of family, friends and hospital staff who helped me through the darkest moments of my journey to those who surrounded me on that day at John O' Groats, I had only gained. My life was richer and fuller than it had ever been before.

"MY DARREN" BY JULIE EDWARDS

I have found this extremely difficult to write. It has been so hard to record my thoughts and feelings about the events of Saturday 6 August 2016, a date that changed my life, as well as Darren's, in an instant. When I answered the phone that day, it was my daughter Eve on the other end. I knew from her tone that she was upset and, on reflection, it must have been so hard for her to break the terrible news to me. I can't recall exactly how she told me but the three words that I heard so clearly were "**Darren**", "**accident**" and "**hospital**". After ending the call, I struggled to piece together exactly what had been said. For some reason, I thought Darren had been involved in a car accident and taken to the Royal Shrewsbury Hospital.

Very shortly afterwards Doctor Ed from A&E at the Royal Stoke University Hospital rang and informed me that Darren had been involved in a climbing accident and had been brought to the hospital by helicopter. He told me Darren had received a "*significant*" injury but stressed that it was not life-threatening. He asked me to take my time in travelling to the hospital safely and that he would speak to me in more depth once I arrived. He let me speak briefly to Darren and I do remember saying, "What have you been up to?"

Once Eve had arrived home, we set off on the 35-mile

journey to the hospital, along with Darren and Eve's dad and my mum. It was late evening by then and driving in darkness along the winding country roads seemed endless. We were unfamiliar with the Newcastle-under-Lyme area and its huge hospital site and spent what seemed an age trying to find the car park nearest to A&E. For the first time in my life, I abandoned the car without getting a ticket as I felt so frustrated and agitated making sense of the Pay and Display machine with instructions to pay for however long we were planning to be there: 1 hour, 2 hours, 24 hours – who knew?

When I finally saw Darren in a cubicle in A&E my first and overwhelming sense was one of relief. "Hello Mum, I'm so sorry," he said. At that stage, I still didn't know the full extent of his injuries but all that mattered was that he was *ALIVE*; he was conscious, and he was speaking to me normally and squeezing my hand. He was still "My Darren". Nothing else mattered at that moment.

It was only when Doctor Ed spoke to us in the Relatives' Room that the seriousness of his injuries became apparent. I asked if Darren would be able to walk again. "Unlikely," came the reply. I was almost functioning on auto pilot by then; I felt numb and kept thinking it was all just a bad dream. Any minute I would wake up and all would be well. It was so hard for me to process what was happening and deal with the emotions of those around me too. I knew I had to dig deep to remain strong for Darren's sake and that of my daughter Eve. Going to pieces would help neither of them. A mother's instinct to protect her children at all costs, I guess. Over and over I just remember feeling so incredibly thankful that Darren hadn't died, particularly after hearing the full horror of what had happened from his best friend Matt, who had been rock climbing with him that day. Ellie, Darren's girlfriend, and Matt's family were also at the hospital and were so very supportive of us.

Darren was eventually transferred to the Critical Care Unit, and we were told spinal surgery would take place early the next day. We drove home exhausted and in silence at around 4 am Sunday. It was approximately 12 hours before I would see Darren again, post-surgery.

Hanging around in the waiting room later that Sunday was almost unbearable, and I finally gave way to tiredness and tears. Wendy, the lovely receptionist in Critical Care, noticed my distress and kindly opened a small and more private Relatives' Room with comfy sofas. She brought some pillows and a welcome cup of tea and told me to try and get some rest; she would let us know when Darren was back from surgery and able to have visitors. Subsequently, Wendy also arranged for a free car parking permit and organised for me to stay close by for three nights in hospital accommodation reserved for the relatives of those in Critical Care. This accommodation was a real godsend as it saved the long drive back and forth. Eve was able to come and stay with me for two of those nights and we were a great comfort to each other.

There are two memories of Darren's week in Critical Care that will always stay with me. Firstly, when the staff wheeled his bed, plus attached monitors, out of the emergency exit into the fresh air at his request. It was so uplifting to see the smile on his face and the colour return to his cheeks as he felt the cool, fresh air on his body, and was able to look up at the sky again. Secondly, when a member of staff from the Spinal Injuries Ward spoke to me quietly while I sat beside a sleeping Darren. She reassured me that, although serious, his level of injury was such that he would be able to lead an independent life and he would be able to father children in the future.

When Darren transferred to the Robert Jones and Agnes Hunt Orthopaedic Hospital in Oswestry, so began a real rollercoaster of emotions. The six weeks of total bed rest was the hardest time to keep him in good spirits; I felt frightened that it might drive him to despair. The wonderful staff on Wrekin Ward were happy to regularly wheel him into a shady spot in the courtyard just outside his room; the summer weather was kind, and he was able to get outside most days. I hated having to say goodbye each time I left for home, knowing his low points were at night time when visitors had gone. Thankfully, the staff had the wisdom to put Darren in a room with another young man called Tim, who was good company for him and like-minded with a positive mental attitude. They both shared a similar bond and Darren made a friend who knew exactly how he was feeling.

As I write, it is now four months down the line and Darren is almost ready for discharge from the hospital and the many challenges that will lie ahead. The other day I watched a baby crawling around in a restaurant. It took me back to when Darren had been that age and I had willed him to take his first tentative steps as an anxious first-time parent, thinking, "How will he ever manage it?" He figured it out then and I believe he will do so again. I will still be there to catch him if needed.

The human body is a wonderful machine that we largely take for granted until something happens that changes our perspective. I watched the 2016 Paralympics in a whole new light. The people who competed had overcome their disabilities to represent their country in a worldwide sporting event. Their stories were so fascinating and inspirational. My son's life has taken a different path from the one I had envisioned for him, but he has shown so much courage and determination throughout his ordeal. I am so incredibly proud to be his Mum.

Finally, as we go forward into the future together, I give thanks to God for keeping Darren safe from death that day by putting Matt close enough to save him from falling any further, and for remaining calm when it mattered. God has also given me the strength to bear all that has happened since and truly blessed me and my family with the love, support and friendship of so many wonderful people along the way.

"LOOKING UP" BY MATT LUXTON

We had planned a two-week expedition to Iceland in August of 2016, where we aimed to explore the island and discover some of Iceland's best climbing and mountaineering routes. I had just come back home to Oswestry for summer leave from the military so, the weekend before we flew, we decided to head to North Wales to warm up our climbing skills. We decided to head to Llangollen, to an old quarry called World's End. It was a perfect day; sunshine, no wind and, in the hills with my best friend, I couldn't be happier.

Skip forward a few hours. We had been climbing all day, doing moderate routes, nothing too tricky, and mixing it up with some lead climbing, abseiling and top roping. We had decided to do one last tricky climb in the middle tier of the quarry, and then head down to finish off the day. Darren led, and the ascent was, in his words, "The hardest thing I have ever climbed", so when he got to the top, we were both exhilarated from meeting the challenge. But that exhilaration was to be cut short.

Darren was about to start abseiling from the top of the cliff when his footing collapsed beneath him and he fell, hit a ledge, and then rolled off the top of the steep rockface, plummeting ten meters straight onto his back. I was waiting at the bottom so didn't see any of this. Instead, I heard the sudden cry of my name "MATT!" and, looking up, saw him falling before hearing an almighty THUD as he hit the ground. It was one of those moments where everything happened so fast, but at the same time I felt like I was watching something in slow motion. The ground was sloped downward so Darren immediately started to roll downhill. Seeing him rolling, with no apparent control over his body, I immediately knew he was in a bad way. I sprinted towards him and slid down the slope to catch him and stop the roll. Thankfully, I got to him in time because he was heading for another life-threatening drop, in which case he would have undoubtedly been killed.

As a Royal Navy Clearance Diver, I have had extensive, professional training and have been deployed all over the world so when I say the training kicks in, it does. However, the moment I had stopped him from falling and heard him say, "Matt, I can't feel my legs!" It felt like I'd been shot in the gut. I knew I couldn't move him, even though he was uncomfortable and in pain but, once he was still, I checked him over. I could see blood, so immediately thought the worst, but, amazingly, his head and neck were fine. The blood had come from a long cut on his arm as he had landed in a thorn bush. I carefully removed all the branches from underneath him and from his arm, undid his harness, and very carefully removed his climbing gear from beneath him.

Luckily for us a couple climbing higher up had heard what had happened and immediately came to help. I told the woman to ring 999 while I was trying to reassure Darren and prevent him from slipping any further down the mountainside. After what seemed like an eternity, but was only about 30 minutes, the Mountain Rescue Team arrived on the scene. The HM

Coastguard helicopter arrived first, and the winchman came down and immediately went to work, asking Darren questions and fully assessing him before the rescue team's doctor arrived. The helicopter disappeared briefly at this point. When the doctor arrived minutes later, he gave Darren some morphine and tried to make him more comfortable by cutting and removing his harness. By the time the other MRT guys had arrived, I took a step back while they went to work on Darren.

It was at this point that I realized we were meant to have been home by now, so I called home and my dad answered the phone. I guess because of the adrenaline, shock and surprise of it all I hadn't been able to process what had happened, until the exact moment my dad answered. "Hey Matt, what's up?" At that moment it all hit me, and I could not control my emotions. I just started crying and whimpering on the phone to him, trying to explain what had happened. It's a feeling I've never had before, and it was uncontrollable and overwhelming. It was, without a doubt, the most awful moment of my life.

The MRT guys are unbelievably good at what they do, and I've never seen anything so impressive. The pilot, hovering meters from the rock face and about fifteen meters above us, was a sight to behold. After they had moved Darren onto a spinal board and eventually winched him up, it took a couple of attempts for the rescue helicopter to hover in the correct position, as the wind had picked up. At this point, I was covering Darren with his jacket to protect him from the cold downdraught of the helicopter. I gathered all his kit and was escorted down to where my car was parked. The MRT guys offered me a lift back home, but I declined. As I pulled up on the drive at home my family were all there waiting for me, which again opened the floodgates. After I gathered myself together, I explained what had happened, and we got into dad's car to the Critical Care Unit at Stoke Hospital. For the next few weeks, I would be spending my time there, and then at the Midlands Centre for Spinal Injuries.

Printed in Great Britain
by Amazon

32989925R00115